On the SOCIOLOGY of DEVIANT BEHAVIOR

By Richard E. Hilbert
& Charles W. Wright

NEW FORUMS

NEW FORUMS PRESS INC.

Published in the United States of America
by New Forums Press, Inc. 1018 S. Lewis St.
Stillwater, OK 74074
www.newforums.com

Copyright © 2020 by Richard E. Hilbert & Charles W. Wright

All rights reserved. No part of this publication may be reproduced or transmitted in any form or by any means, electronic or mechanical, including photocopy, or any information storage or retrieval system, without permission in writing from the publisher.

Library of Congress Cataloging-in-Publication Data Pending

This book may be ordered in bulk quantities at discount from New Forums Press, Inc., P.O. Box 876, Stillwater, OK 74076 [Federal I.D. No. 73 1123239]. Printed in the United States of America.

ISBN 10: 1-58107-350-X
ISBN 13: 978-1-58107-350-8

Contents

I. Introduction v

II. The Theory of Anomie as an Explanation for Deviance in America: Its Development and Implication for Change 1

III. Representations of Merton's Theory of Anomie 93

IV. Contrasting Conceptions of Deviance in Sociology: Functionalism and Labeling Theory 107

V. Value Implications of the Functional Theory of Deviance 129

VI. Durkheim and Quinney on the Inevitability of Crime: A Comparative Theoretical Analysis 157

VII. Adaptive Structures and the Problem of Order 179

VIII. The Command Economy as an Adaptive Structure 193

Author Biographies 215

Introduction

The following compendium consists of seven chapters. All of these statements focus upon the theoretical developments and controversies associated with the theory of crime and/or deviance that developed in the United States in the mid-to-late twentieth century. The theories and controversy remain salient in the sociological analysis of deviance, crime, and delinquency to this day.

The first chapter, "Anomie as an Explanation for Deviance and Social Unrest in Societies of the American Type," authored by R.E. Hilbert, was written in response to a call for papers in celebration of the American Bi-Centennial by the University of Oklahoma Press. The volume was published in 1976. The work is a history, analysis, and contribution to the development of the theory of anomie in America and related theoretical developments. Hilbert calls attention to the fact that a "disturbing phenomenon," deviance and social unrest in modern societies, is a result not of some alien intrusion into social life, but rather is a result of essential features of such societies. Thus, the source cannot be eliminated without making important changes in the structure of such societies.

Although your authors are not inclined to advocate any particular program of social change (within the confines of this discourse), in this collection of work, we do describe the more obvious possibilities (alternative social structures), along with the "costs" associated with adopting one or the other. The implication of the analysis suggests that the "problem" of high rates of crime and other types of deviance persists because we are unwilling to make the institutional changes necessary to eliminate the sources of the pressure to engage in such conduct.

The second chapter in the collection, "Representations of Merton's Theory of Anomie," was originally published in 1979 by *The American Sociologist* (Hilbert and Wright). This work is an exposition and analysis of the way Robert Merton's famous statement of "Social Structure and Anomie" (1937) has been interpreted by professional sociologists. As such, the chapter is an exercise in the "Sociology of Sociology." We find that the interpretation of this statement by American sociologists is largely skewed in an ideologically liberal direction and that presentation and discussion of the more deeply critical elements of the theory are rare.

We also focus on the concept of the social structure itself in this statement. In examining structural alternatives, which might reduce the strains intrinsic to societies of the American type, we compare alternative social structures. In so doing, the concept of social structure is thrown into sharp relief and the comparative analysis of such structures may be presented with greater clarity and thereby made more transparent. We also compare the various structures with respect to their impact on the productivity levels and resources that flow from the differentiated structural forms. This focus permits us to establish the significance of bureaucratic/meritocratic institutions not only in terms of the valued productivity and efficiency that they foster, but also the social costs, which the unbridled competition that they ultimately demand imposes upon traditional relationships: This includes a negative effect on the family and friendship, as well as individual health, and the social order.

In the third chapter, "Value Implications of the Functional theory of Deviance" (Wright and Hilbert, 1980), we continue to focus upon the theory of anomie and related theoretical systems, but we hone in on the implications of social theory on values and beliefs. Specifically, we argue that "critical criminology" is no more radical in its implications for social change than is functional analysis. The primary difference is that the raison d'être of critical criminology is the advocacy of social change while "academic sociology" is analytical and insists upon suspension of one's values and beliefs in the pursuit of "scientific" analysis. Here, we focus on the radical implications that are implied, if not announced, by the functional theories of deviance. We also argue, in agreement with Alvin Gouldner (1970), that the critique of societies of the American type, embedded within functional theories of deviance, is fundamental.

In the fourth and fifth chapters, "Contrasting Conceptions of Deviance in Sociology: Functionalism and Labeling Theory" (Wright and Randall, 1978), and "Durkheim and Quinney on the Inevitability of Crime: A Comparative Theoretical Analysis" (Hilbert and Wright, 1982) we move to a different level of theoretical analysis. Our objective is to display the material significance of the underlying frame of reference or "conceptual scheme" in the development of systems of substantive (explanatory) theory. Primarily, this effort involves an analysis of the language of the theory. In pursuing this objective we focus on the meaning of and relations between the primary concepts, e.g., "norm" or alternatively "rule," and the logical and empirical relations between the conceptual elements of the scheme. This approach, following Thomas Kuhn's method in *The Structure of Scientific Revolutions* (1964), aims to elaborate and interpret the key concepts that undergird the substantive conclusions of a theory. For example, concepts like rules, norms, crime, deviance, society, power, law, guilt, segmentation, integration, and consensus, etc. are not taken for granted; rather they are subjected to an in-depth analysis in an effort to understand the basics of the perspective or "point of view" from which substantive/explanatory theory is ultimately derived. In short, our aim is to reveal that at each stage of the development of sociological understanding and knowledge "theory matters."

The six and seventh chapters in the collection should be read together as one piece. The first, "Adaptive Structures and the Problem of Order" (C. Hart 2009, *A Collection of Essays in Honour of Talcott Parsons*), develops and elaborates the concept of "adaptive structures" and develops its utility in understanding how social order obtains in modern societies. The second, "The Command Economy as an Adaptive Structure" (Hilbert and Wright, 2017), applies this concept to a substantive, historical example.

In chapter six, we note that an "adaptive structure" involves an "emergent" or longstanding pattern within the society that is oppositional and subordinate to the dominant institutionalized pattern. Ironically, although the adaptive pattern is understood to be "functional" in that it deals with real or imagined threats to the maintenance of dominant elements of the societal structure, it is in opposition to the dominant pattern. A recent example of such an emergent pattern in the American society, which, it is believed, will enhance the chances of survival of the dominant institutions of the society, is the so-called "Patriot Act." This law deeply offends the privacy values that are a central component of the American way of life, like Constitutional limits on search and seizure. Nonetheless, the oppositional pattern expressed in the Patriot Act is given widespread support by Americans, apparently because it is viewed as necessary to deflect fundamental threats to the society as a whole.

The necessity of such "adaptability" is perhaps originally noted by Durkheim in his discussion of "The Normal and the Pathological" (1938, *The Rules of Sociological Method*). In that work, Durkheim urges that a society that is "inflexible" is in danger of going out of existence because of the collectivity's refusal to compromise or depart from its cherished values in the face of external or internal threats to societal survival. In this case, the societal view appears to be something like "better dead than red." Durkheim makes his position clearer stating:

> [I]t is no longer possible today to dispute the fact that law and morality vary from one social type to the next, nor that they change within the same type if the *conditions of life are modified.* But, in order that these transformations may be possible, the collective sentiments at the basis of morality must not be hostile to change, and consequently must have but moderate energy. If they were too strong they would no longer be plastic. Every pattern is an obstacle to new patterns, to the extent that the first pattern is inflexible. *Emphasis added* (Rules, p. 70)

In chapter seven, we attempt to illustrate further the utility of the concept "adaptive structure" by drawing on historical descriptions of the features of the American "command economy," in place during World War II. This "adaptation," in the American socio-economic system, was initially instituted in face of the threat posed to the United States by Nazi Germany and Fascistic Japan. The "command economy" departed in fundamental ways from the highly valued structures of the "competitive market." Regardless, the American people and their representatives believed that this departure from long-held core values was necessary in order to win the war and protect the "American way of life." In addition, we also analyze the tensions generated by the co-existence of alternative and oppositional social structures within the same society. Finally, we give brief attention to the means by which the adaptive structure might be insulated so that the "adaptive tail" does not come to wag the "dominant institutional dog" and thereby effectuate a social change.

We hope and believe that this compilation will be valuable to professors and students of upper-level undergraduate courses and those pursuing advanced sociological degrees and careers in sociology, as well as providing a sharper understanding of the comparative analysis of sociological theory.

Last, given our decades-long interest and participation in the scholarship associated with the discipline of sociology, many colleagues and friends have given us assistance and support. We cannot thank them all here. However, we hope that at the appropriate time we exhibited that appreciation, which we felt and they deserved. With respect to the project at hand, we wish to express special appreciation to Doug Dollar, who kindly took on the task of bringing the work to publication and distribution through the New Forums publishing house; Bill Riggins, who guided us in locating an appropriate publisher; and, Laurie Lucas, who assumed the tedious task of copy editing the entire manuscript. The work simply would never have come to publication without their assistance.

In conclusion, we wish to show our appreciation to our wives, Lois Hilbert and Laurie Lucas, by dedicating the work to them. Thank you! REH and CW

The Theory of Anomie as an Explanation for Deviance in America: Its Development and Implication for Change

By R. E. Hilbert

It is now a rather widely accepted fact that the United States of America, the most advanced of the great industrial societies, is beset with enormous problems in the areas of crime and social unrest. In addition to alarmingly high rates of adult criminal behavior and juvenile delinquency, there is the constant threat of riots in our urban centers and challenges to the social order from virtually every minority group within our borders.[1] Less widely accepted, but equally important, is the fact that, in varying degrees, these problems have been with us since the very beginning of America as a nation state. Although the data are not always reliable, it appears that throughout the nineteenth century, the high rate of violence within our borders is unmatched within the stable democracies.[2] The situation with respect to offenses against property and corruption in government throughout the

---

Previously published in *Issues and Ideas in America,* Benjamin J. Taylor and Thurman J. White, Eds. Norman, OK: University of Oklahoma Press.

same period is no less appalling. Writing over a hundred years ago, the poet Whitman, generally regarded as an optimist, had this to say about the American scene:

> Never was there, perhaps, more hollowness at heart than at present, and here in the United States. Genuine belief seems to have left us. The underlying principles of the States are not believed in (for all this hectic glow, and these melodramatic screamings), nor is humanity itself believ'd in. What penetrating eye does not everywhere see through the mask? The spectacle is appalling. We live in an atmosphere of hypocrisy throughout. The men believe not in the women, nor the women in the men. A scournful superciliousness rules in our literature....The depravity of the business classes of our country is not less than has been supposed, but infinitely greater. The official services of America, national, state, and municipal, in all their branches and departments, except the judiciary, are saturated in corruption, bribery, falsehood, mal-administration; and the judiciary is tainted. The great cities reek with respectable as well as non-respectable robbery and scoundrelism... (Whitman, 1870).

Introduction

Taken together, these facts about the history and present status of deviance and social unrest in America suggest (to a sociologist, at least) that the source of the problem may very well lie in the organization of American society and, further, that the problematic features of that organization may be among the time-honored features of the American way of life.

The present chapter is concerned with social organization and its impact on deviance and social unrest. However, it is not our aim to review all (or even everything of significance) that has ever been said on the subject. Rather, it is to expose in some detail one important theoretical perspective relating deviance and social unrest to social organization. For a variety of reasons, not the least of which is the author's preoccupation with social theory, there will be no systematic concern with the results of various empirical tests of the theory, of which it might be noted, there are a great many.[3] The emphasis will be on exposing the development of the perspective and its implications for social change as a solution to those consequences of this form of organization that are considered problematic. However, it will quickly become evident that even a self-consciously theoretical work must make some reference to empirical data, if only to illustrate the utility of a particular theoretical point.

Anomie as a theory of deviance may be said to have originated with the publication in 1938 of the now famous article by Robert K. Merton entitled "Social Structure and Anomie."[4] Although the term anomie was used as early as the sixteenth century (Merton, 1957, p. 135), it was not used widely until the latter part of the nineteenth century, when it was reintroduced into the literature by Emile Durkheim.[5] Literally, the term translates as "normlessness," but is conceived today as a condition in human society in which certain of its members develop a lack of respect for the goals of the society, or for the norms which prescribe the legitimate means by which those goals may be pursued, or for both. With respect to the meaning of the term, a great deal more will be said later, in the treatment of those persons who have contributed to the development of the theory. For now, it is sufficient to say that the concept has earned a significant place in the frame of reference of the professional sociologist.

The recentness of the particular theoretical development under review may puzzle many readers. It seems to be related to two modes of thought which were characteristic of much social theory prior to the twentieth century. The first was a tendency to see deviance as a product of something basic to man's nature. This is in contrast to the view prevalent today, which ascribes a great deal of causal significance to the organization of the system within which the deviance takes place. According to the earlier view, society played a part, but it was seen as a mechanism by which the nature of man was brought under control. Should deviance break out, according to this view, society might be said to be responsible, in so far as it failed to bring the motivation under control, but the motivation to commit deviant acts was believed to be present at birth or to develop naturally as the actor matures. The mode of thought involved here may well be a variant of the assumption in early Christian thinking that men are born with a propensity to sin. The second was a tendency to think that only evil causes evil; that evil consequences invariably have evil precedents.[6] Given this way of thinking, it was impossible to conclude that a condition defined as evil might be the result of one that is defined as good.

As will be seen, the theory of anomie runs counter to both these modes of thought: It holds that deviant motivation is often system-generated and thus implies (in the case of deviance in America) that a condition defined as evil may be a consequence of one that is defined as good, the American Way of Life. Moreover, it holds that the features of the system which are responsible cannot easily be altered or cast aside, because they lie at the heart of that system.

It should be evident at this point that this commentary is as much a critique of the American way of life as it is an historical treatment of the development of a body of theory. Moreover, in view of the fact that the ideas involved have come mainly from American sociologists, it may be said to be a theory about America by Americans. Its inclusion in the bicentennial collection is therefore particularly appropriate.

The subject matter of this chapter is divided into five parts. The first part is given over to the views of Emile Durkheim on the sources of anomie in modern societies and on certain of its consequences. Next is a rather detailed treatment of the reformulation of Durkheim's original ideas by Robert K. Merton. The third part explores the more significant contributions to the further development of the theory of three authors: Talcott Parsons, Albert K. Cohen, and Richard Cloward (writing with Lloyd Ohlin). Fourth, there are introduced several additional considerations which, in the opinion of this author, contribute to the further development of the theory. Finally, we take up the question of the implications of the theory for social reform, on the assumption that the consequences of anomie, in some cases at least, are sufficiently problematic to justify a consideration of social reform as a way of reducing the rates at which they now occur.

The Contributions of Emile Durkheim
Anomie and the Division of Labor

Durkheim (1964b) introduced the concept of anomie in his first major work, *The Division of Labor in Society*, published in 1893. His thesis in that work may be seen as a highly polemical attack on several bodies of thought in the intellectual tradition of his day. One of these was a position, deriving from the work of Comte, which stressed the importance for social order of what Durkheim referred to as a "collective conscience," a set of specific moral norms and supporting sentiments with respect to which there is a high degree of consensus. Another was a conclusion, associated with the utilitarian individualism of the political economists and English philosophers, concerning the integrating effects in modern societies of individual contracts. An understanding of Durkheim's early contribution to the theory of anomie requires that we examine his attacks on both these bodies of thought.

Durkheim readily agreed that a high degree of consensus on specific moral norms is necessary for social order, so long as the generalization is limited to the simpler societies, i.e., those that are relatively undifferentiated in terms of the division of labor. He agreed also with those critics of industrial societies who argued that, as the division of labor advances, we can expect the degree of consensus relative to the "collective conscience" to decline, if for no other reason than that the division of labor emphasizes differences rather than similarities in the way men think and act. However, he did not agree with the conclusion often drawn by these critics that the decline in the "collective conscience" necessarily leads to disorder. Rather, he believed that, in the "normal" case, advances in the division of labor lead to a new form of solidarity, one based on the complementary relationships which develop when work roles are specialized and men are functionally interdependent. Durkheim referred to this new form of solidarity as "organic solidarity," and much of his early work had to do with its character and development in human society.

It was in connection with his effort to expose this new form of solidarity that Durkheim was moved to attack the utilitarian individualism of the political economists and English philosophers. He argued that integration in advanced industrial societies was not, as suggested in utilitarian individualism, the result of a network of essentially economic contracts between formally free individuals in a market. On the contrary, such contracts would be quite impossible without prior commitment to a set of constraining norms or "rules of the game." In other words, the existence of contractual relations, according to Durkheim, presupposes a normative structure without which the formation of such relations could not proceed in an orderly fashion. Above all, a normative structure cannot be explained as an outgrowth of contractual relations, if the former is a necessary condition for the emergence of the latter.

Thus it is clear from the context of Durkheim's argument with the utilitarians, that he believed the division of labor leads to a new solidarity, but not simply by making men interdependent or by forcing them to deal with each other in a market. Rather, it does so by creating a new morality. In his own words (1964b, p. 406):

> [I]f the division of labor produces solidarity, it is not only because it makes each individual an *exchangist*, as the economists say; it is because it creates among men an entire system of rights and duties which link them together in a durable way. Just as social similitudes [in the simpler societies] give rise to law and a morality which protect them, so the division of labor [in modern societies] gives rise to rules which assure pacific and regular concourse of divided functions.

But if Durkheim was critical of utilitarian individualism as an accurate description of the basis for solidarity in modern societies, he was inclined to give it a prominent place in the thinking of modern men and in the development of the division of labor itself. Indeed, it may be seen as providing the moral support for the individualization which the division of labor involves. Particularly important in this regard is the "cult of the individual," a set of beliefs about the dignity and worth of the individual which had its origins in the Enlightenment and which figured significantly in the philosophical justification for the French Revolution.

Durkheim recognized that such beliefs may be conceived as an element within the common conscience, but—and here he returns to the dominant theme in his treatment of the subject—they contribute nothing to the development of solidarity.

> It is thus, if one wishes, a common cult, but it is possible only by the ruin of all others, and, consequently, cannot produce the same effects as this multitude of extinguished beliefs. There is no compensation for that. Moreover, if it is common in so far as the community partakes of it, it is individual in its object. If it turns all wills towards the same end, this end is not social. It thus occupies a completely exceptional place in the collective conscience. It is still from society that it takes all its force, but it is not to society that it attaches us; it is to ourselves. Hence it does not constitute a true social link (1964b, p. 172).

At this stage in the development of his argument, Durkheim found himself in a kind of bind. Having concluded that the position of the utilitarian individualists concerning the integrating effects of individual contracts was naive (that, in fact, the existence of contracts presupposes a morality without which such contracts could not proceed) and, further, that advances in the division of labor gave rise to this morality (while at the same time undermining the basis for solidarity prior to such advances), Durkheim was at pains to explain the fact that conflict and social unrest are so often present in societies in which the division of labor has progressed to an advanced state. Indeed, it was precisely because of this fact that many critics of industrialism had concluded that the division of labor was the factor primarily responsible for the conflict and social unrest in industrial societies.

But Durkheim had an answer: He argued that where conflict and social unrest are associated with advances in the division of labor, it is because the latter has progressed more rapidly than the morality necessary for its regulation. It was in relation to this condition that Durkheim first used the term *anomie*. Translated literally, anomie means normlessness, but in the context of *The Division of Labor* it refers to a condition in which relations between specialists are insufficiently regulated to produce functional unity (the essence of organic solidarity). Interestingly, this is precisely the kind of condition one would expect to find if men were in fact related to one another in the manner described by the utilitarian individualists; that is, in terms of individual contracts and nothing more. It may be argued that in the absence of such regulation men could be expected to operate in terms of norms of efficiency in the formation of contractual relations. Such norms do not preclude the use of coercive power and, depending upon the circumstances, may actually lead to the use of such power. As will be seen, it is precisely this implication of Durkheim's thesis which became the cornerstone of one aspect of Merton's formulation of the theory, that aspect having to do with anomie as a function of the emphasis on utilitarianism in modern societies.[7]

Durkheim referred to a condition in which there is insufficient regulation between specialists as the "anomic division of labor." A good illustration of such a condition is the conflict between capital and wage labor, which Durkheim saw as widespread and as having serious consequences for the development of class conflict. Nevertheless, he was optimistic about the eventual outcome. In time, he believed, norms adequate to the task of regulating such relations would develop, because they were needed. For Durkheim, at least in this stage of his intellectual development, this was the way all such norms developed, in response to the need for them.

But although optimistic concerning the eventual development of adequate normative regulation of the relations between specialties, Durkheim was concerned about the quality of the norms that were under development. Because of the unequal distribution of power ("external inequality"), especially in the relations between capital and labor, norms might develop which would regularize such relations, but which would be seen as unjust. Durkheim referred to such norms (and the contracts negotiated in terms of them) as the "forced division of labor." They are unjust because those who are subject to them do not always get what they deserve.

> If one class of society is obliged, in order to live, to take any price for its services, while another can abstain from such action thanks to resources at its disposal which, however, are not necessarily due to

any social superiority, the second has an unjust advantage over the first at law (1964b, p. 384).

More important for understanding his contribution to the development of the modern theory of anomie, Durkheim was convinced that the "forced division of labor" was inherently unstable. The individualism which underlies the whole process of specialization fosters a tendency toward individual self-fulfillment which can be held in check only at great cost to the society, in terms of conflict and social unrest. Indeed, revolutions have been known to spring from precisely this source of instability. In the very beginning of his discussion of the subject, he states (1964b, p. 374):

> It is not sufficient that there be rules, however, for sometimes the rules themselves are the cause of evil. This is what occurs in class-wars. The institution of classes and of castes constitutes an organization of the division of labor, and it is a strictly regulated organization, although it often is a source of dissention. The lower classes not being, or no longer being, satisfied with the role which was devolved upon them from custom or by law aspire to functions which are closed to them and seek to dispossess those who are exercising these functions. Thus civil wars arise which are due to the manner in which labor is distributed.

Several observations are worth noting before closing the discussion of Durkheim's early contribution to the theory of anomie. For Durkheim, a phenomenon is to be considered "normal" if it is an inevitable consequence of a particular species of society; "abnormal" if it is not. In *The Division of Labor*, anomie is treated as an abnormal phenomenon, an imperfection in the state of organic solidarity which can be expected to disappear as the evolution of regulatory norms proceeds. He was particularly concerned with demonstrating that it was not an inevitable consequence of advances in the division of labor. Thus in his early work, at least, Durkheim appeared to be a critic of the industrial way of life, but an optimistic one. Second, in the context of The *Division of Labor*, anomie is a condition in which there is inadequate regulation of the activities of the persons involved, *including the means which they use in relating to one another.* This is not the emphasis given to the concept of anomie in his later work, specifically in *Suicide*, as we shall see. Third, given this concept of anomie, it would not be appropriate to see it as a source of deviant behavior, however undesirable he may have considered the consequences, but rather as a defect in the solidarity of the emerging social order—in today's language, a kind of social disorganization.

In summary, then, Durkheim's early contribution to the theory of anomie had to do, first, with calling attention to the fact that society is a moral order, and that the form which that order takes varies considerably, depending on the level of specialization or the division of labor. It had to do, second, with showing that the conditions described as ideal by the utilitarian individualists could not possibly provide the solidarity necessary for the persistence of a complex industrial society, and that without some kind of normative structure to control the use of coercive means, life would approximate the Hobbesian "war of all against all." Third, it had to do with the observation that in the development of the division of labor in human societies, the morality necessary for its regulation sometimes fails to develop, with anomie as the result. Finally, it had to do with the existence and significance for solidarity of "external inequality" (of power). Thus even when regulatory rules develop, solidarity may be impaired if the rules in question have been developed unilaterally as a result of this inequality. Called the "forced division of labor," such a system of rules is inherently unstable because it does not take account of the pressure generated by the ideology of individualism, with its emphasis on self-fulfillment through the development of one's talents and abilities.

Anomie and Suicide

Durkheim's early work on the division of labor in human society is the foundation upon which the bulk of his later writing rests. Even his work on suicide should be seen as an elaboration of the theme set out in his early work on the division of labor.

All of the "suicidal currents" with which he was concerned in *Suicide* are consequences of the moral orders introduced in *The Division of Labor*. Moreover, the substance of his critique of industrial society in *Suicide* extended and developed ideas which were treated originally in his earlier work.

Durkheim's study of suicide is significant in several respects apart from the substance of his critique of industrial society. First, it is a classic example of a type of approach to the understanding of social life which has come to be associated with the discipline of sociology, namely, the analysis of variations in the rates of social phenomena. So common is this type of analysis in sociology today that it is sometimes referred to as *the* "sociological" approach. It contrasts sharply with the "clinical" approach, which is concerned with incidence. In the latter, an attempt is made to explain why one person rather than another behaves in a given way.[8] Second, it explains suicide in the context of the larger society rather than by reference to variables on the level of biology or individual psychology. Durkheim was among the first sociologists to reject the tendency toward reductionism in psychology, political economy, and political philosophy. Social facts, though not unrelated to biological and psychological facts, have a reality of their own.

> It has often appeared that these social phenomena, because of their extreme complexity, were either inhospitable to science or could be subject to it only when reduced to their elemental conditions, either psychic or organic, that is, only when stripped of their proper nature. We have, on the contrary, undertaken to establish that it is possible to treat them scientifically without removing any of their distinctive characteristics. We have even refused to identify the immateriality of psychological phenomena; we have, furthermore, refused to reabsorb it, with the Italian school, into the general properties of organized matter (1964a, pp. 144-145).

It should be clear, then, that Durkheim's approach, on the level of theory as well as methodology, is pre-eminently sociological. This will become more apparent as we expose his work on suicide.

In general terms, the thesis in *Suicide* is that rates of suicide vary as a function of system-generated "suicidal currents" to which the members of a society are subject, depending on the positions they occupy. These currents are called "altruism," "egoism" and "anomie." Suicide resulting primarily from any one of the above currents is given the name of that current. For example, suicide resulting primarily from "egoism" is given the name of "egoistic suicide." There is full recognition, however, that for a given category of persons, two or more currents may be operating, sometimes at cross-purposes, to determine the rate of suicide for that category.

Altruistic suicide, according to Durkheim, tends to occur when the interests of the group are so important to the individual that his private interests, including his own life, become secondary considerations. The classic example of altruistic suicide, as one might expect, is the soldier who knowingly gives his life for his country, although there are other examples as well to which one might point: The Hindu woman who kills herself upon the death of her husband and the Ashanti officer who kills himself upon the death of his chief. Durkheim was particularly fascinated with the statistics on suicide among military personnel, because they presented striking examples of support for his thesis. For instance, the rates for military personnel are higher than for similar civilian groups. This is true in times of peace as well as in times of war. To refute the argument that the rates of suicide among military personnel are high because of the hardships of military life, Durkheim pointed out that the rates are higher for officers than for enlisted men, whose lot is generally a more difficult one. Moreover, rates of suicide increase with length of service, which is exactly what one would *not* expect, if it may be assumed that the first few years of service are always the more difficult to endure.

At the other extreme from altruistic suicide is egoistic suicide. It was conceived as resulting from an inordinately low degree of concern for group interests and thus for precisely those elements of social organization which give meaning to life. Thus if altruistic suicide results from a situation in which death has too much meaning to offset the advantages of life, egoistic suicide results from a situation in which life has too little meaning to offset the advantages of death. Durkheim supported his thesis concerning egoistic suicide by reference to data drawn from a number of areas of social life. His analysis of the statistics in the area of domestic relations, for example, showed that married persons tend to have lower rates than single persons, or those who have been widowed or divorced. Moreover, differences in this regard tend to increase in proportion to the size of the family unit. The significant variable, of course, is commitment to group interests and the meaning which such commitment provides.

In his treatment of egoistic suicide, Durkheim spent a great deal of time with the differences in rates of suicide between various religious groups. His analysis in this regard is particularly instructive, because it points up the fact that there are special cases, of which Protestantism is one, in which it is not just the absence of norms favoring full participation in the group, but the *presence* of norms favoring autonomy which is responsible for the low level of integration. In developing his argument, he noted first that Protestants have significantly higher rates than Catholics, and that the relationship holds true when other variables are held constant. He then pointed out that for the Catholic, religious truth and proper conduct are prescribed by the church, so that the question of salvation can be solved by compliance with church doctrine. For the Protestant, the situation is quite different. The ultimate judge of truth and proper conduct is not the church, but the individual. The net result is freedom from the obligation to comply with church doctrine, but it is a freedom which enjoins him to make his own decisions on matters of religion and morality. Thus, in so far as he is faithful, the Protestant must bear a burden of responsibility which, in the case of the Catholic, can be shifted to the church. It is this burden, of course, that creates the strain disposing him to suicide.[9]

Durkheim's discussion of the impact of religious individualism on egoistic suicide is instructive in another sense as well. It is clear from the context of that discussion that the ethic of individualism, of which religious individualism is but one specific case, is perhaps the most significant variable affecting the low degree of integration in industrial society. It might be noted that his views on this subject are so strong that it would not be going too far to say that Durkheim's treatment of egoistic suicide has all the earmarks of a polemic against unfettered individualism. Later we shall see that the same kind of point can be made about his treatment of anomic suicide.

The third of the types of suicide discussed by Durkheim is anomic suicide. As with the others, it is conceived to be the result of a certain state of the social order, in this case anomie.[10] In his discussion of the sources of anomie, Durkheim relied heavily on certain facts about the variation of rates of suicide by stages of the business cycle. He noted that the rate of suicide increases during periods of unusual prosperity as well as during periods of depression. The fact that the rate goes up during depression is not particularly surprising; common sense might suggest that disappointment and suffering are likely to follow from financial loss. What is surprising is that it also goes up during periods of unusual prosperity, a fact of considerable importance to Durkheim's explanation of its sources.

In working out his explanation, Durkheim observed first that poverty-stricken people are not always upset with their circumstances. From this fact he concluded that even the increase in suicide rates during depressions cannot be explained in terms of the deprivation of economic needs, if such needs are assumed to be absolute and unchanging. On the other hand, if they are conceived to be relative and changing, an explanation which makes reference to the deprivation of economic need might be quite satisfactory. What he concluded, finally, was that the increase in the rate of suicide at the extremes of the business cycle must be the result of disturbances in the relationship between what one expects contingent upon a certain amount of effort, and what one gets. Specifically, he argued that in periods of economic depression, the problem is that the economic status of large numbers of people is out of line with expectations in the area of living standards. In periods of unusual prosperity, on the other hand, the problem is that expectations of large numbers of people tend to get out of line with what is realistically possible. As one authority (Parsons, 1949, p. 335) has put it:

> At both extremes [of the business cycle] the relation between means and ends, between effort and attainment, is upset. The result is a sense of confusion, a loss of orientation. People no longer have a sense of "getting anywhere."

The significance of Durkheim's discussion of suicide during various stages of the business cycle is, first, in calling attention to the fact that to experience success one must not only have access to the means by which goals are reached, but in addition, one must have a clear definition of what the goal is. Above all, the goal cannot be constantly receding. "One does not advance when one walks toward no goal, or—which is the same thing—when the goal is infinity" (Durkheim 1951, p. 248). It is, second, in calling attention to the fact that deprivation is relative to one's aspirations. That is, what is deprivating depends on what one wants, or comes to expect, as a consequence of one's position within the society. In summary, in the context of *Suicide*, anomie results when aspirations are out of line with reality factors in the situation of the actor. It can be eliminated only through the provision of goals which limit the actor to what is realistically possible.

Durkheim's discussion of anomic suicide is significant for another reason as well. It was in his treatment of this subject that he began to see anomie as a normal rather than an abnormal phenomenon in industrial societies. It will be recalled that in *The Division of Labor*, anomie was treated as an abnormal phenomenon, one which is not inevitable in such societies and which in time would be eliminated by the development of normative controls over the relations between specialists. But in *Suicide*, in his discussion of the sources of anomie, he stated that it is sometimes the result of certain general features of the industrial way of life and presumably, therefore, inevitable among the occupants of that way of life. Specifically, he argued that it is related to rapid technological developments and the sudden expansion of markets—conditions which he saw as presenting seemingly unlimited opportunities for the accumulation of wealth. For this reason, "The sphere of trade and industry . . . is actually in a chronic state [of anomie]" (1951, p. 254). In elaborating his point in this regard, he argued as follows (1951, p. 256, emphasis added):

> Now that [the producer] may assume to have almost the entire world as his customer, how could passions accept their former confinement in the face of such limitless prospects? Such is the source of the excitement predominating in this part of society, and which has hence extended to the other parts. There, *the state of crisis and anomie is constant and, so to speak, normal.* From top to bottom of the ladder greed is aroused without knowing where to find ultimate foothold. Nothing can calm it, since its goal is far beyond all it can attain.

Clearly his emphasis has shifted. What was earlier considered an abnormal development, an imperfection in the state of organic solidarity in industrial society, has become an inevitable consequence of the social organization of such a society and thus (by definition) normal. It is the latter theme which pervades the formulations of the theory of anomie which appeared in America, beginning in the late 1930s.

Underlying the discussion of anomie in *Suicide* is an assumption about human nature that should be made explicit. For Durkheim (1951, p. 247-248) *"human activity naturally aspires beyond assignable limits and sets itself unattainable goals."* This view of human nature, which has been called into question in more recent times, reflects a view of man that dominated much Western thought throughout the nineteenth century. According to this view, man is possessed not just with a capacity to crave comfort, luxury, and physical well-being, but with a tendency to do so. The "problem" for society, is to regulate this tendency, for there is nothing in man's biological or psychological makeup that can be expected to perform this function. A stable society, then, is one in which men at all levels within the social order aspire to no more than they can realistically hope to attain, producing a kind of harmony between man and the conditions he faces. Here again, in his treatment of anomie, Durkheim can be seen as striking a major blow at utilitarian individualism, which assumed that there is a direct and universal relationship between increasing prosperity and the advance of human happiness. Clearly he is saying that this is not necessarily the case; that happiness in the face of increasing prosperity is a function of the adequacy of those mechanisms regulating man's aspirations, a variable the utilitarians tended to ignore.

A word needs to be said about the relationship between egoistic and anomic suicide. Both are the result of the "insufficient presence" of society in individuals. But whereas in egoistic suicide there is a deficiency in commitment to collective activity, depriving the individual of meaning, in anomic suicide the deficiency is in commitment to limiting goals, leaving the individual with unrealistic benchmarks, or none at all, for measuring success. Thus, the two types may and do vary independently of one another. Durkheim (1951, p. 258) specifically calls our attention to this fact. *"We may offer society everything social in us, and still be unable to control our desire . . . and vice versa."* Yet it is clear that both types of suicide can be traced to elements within the social organization of modern societies, not the least of which is the division of labor and the ethic of individualism that is associated with it.

In his later work, Durkheim continued to emphasize the inadequacy of psychological or biological reductionism for the development of social theory, stressing instead the importance of explanations of social phenomena which relate those phenomena to the larger society. He also argued that the social structure of modern societies makes it difficult to secure the kind of commitment to the interests of the collectivity which social order requires. This is so because the emphasis on individuality which the division of labor requires heightens the egoistic inclinations of the individual. Moreover, the problem of "restraining horizons" is difficult in such societies, if for no other reason than that they present seemingly unlimited opportunities for the accumulation of wealth. There is, therefore, a tendency toward a lack of regulation of the means which may be used in attaining one's goals (anomie in the context of *The Division of Labor*) and toward a lack of regulation of the tendency to aspire to unrealistic goals (anomie in the context of *Suicide*). Thus, in spite of the optimism concerning the prospects for stability in modern societies expressed in Durkheim's early work, there is every reason to believe that, in the end, he saw in the structure of such societies, features that make the "war of all against all" a constant threat.

The Contributions of Robert K. Merton

Merton's statement of the theory of anomie as an explanation for deviant behavior has been acclaimed by A. K. Cohen (1965, p. 5) as "the most influential single formulation in the sociology of deviance in the last 25 years." That statement, published over 45 years ago, is as unchallenged today as it was when it was made. The original paper is still one of the most frequently quoted in American sociology and has been the basis for literally hundreds of critical commentaries, extensions, and empirical studies on the subject.

Social Structure, Anomie and Deviant Behavior

Merton's version of the theory is a significant advance over Durkheim's original formulation, with respect both to the causes and consequences of anomie. But in developing his ideas, Merton remains solidly within the tradition of sociological thinking which Durkheim did so much to establish: he is concerned with variations in rates of human behavior, rather than in incidence, and he explains those variations within the context of the larger society rather than by reference to variables at the biological or psychological levels of analysis. Thus, following Durkheim, he uses the "sociological approach" and is opposed to any form of reductionism in his treatment of social phenomena. Merton's orientation is made quite explicit in the following excerpt from the introduction to his 1938 paper (1957, p. 132):

> Our primary aim is to discover how some *social structures exert a definite pressure upon certain persons in the society to engage in*

non-conforming rather than conforming conduct. If we can locate groups, not because the human beings comprising them are compounded of distinctive biological tendencies but because they are responding normally to the social situation in which they find themselves, our perspective is sociological. We look at variations in the *rates* of deviant behavior, not at its incidence. Should our quest be at all successful, some forms of deviant behavior will be found to be as psychologically normal as conformist behavior, and the equation of deviant and psychological abnormality will be put into question.

Basic to Merton's thesis is a distinction between "goals" and "means" as elements of the social structure of a society. The distinction between the two, it should be noted, is analytic, so that in concrete situations a particular goal may also be a means to a further goal, but this fact does not make the distinction any less important for theoretical purposes. By "goals" is meant those "purposes and interests" held out as desirable of attainment by a society. They are the things "worth striving for," according to its cultural tradition. By "means," on the other hand, is meant the legitimate ways by which the members of a society, individually or in groups, may pursue the cultural goals. Such ways are defined by the institutions of a society and, depending upon the form of the definition, may be prescribed, preferred, or simply permitted.

Also basic to Merton's thesis is the idea that, although both of these elements of the social structure are present in all human societies, the relations between them are not necessarily constant. In fact, they can and do vary independently of one another. In some societies, for example, the emphasis placed on the attainment of cultural goals may be quite strong, while the emphasis placed on conformity to the norms prescribing legitimate means to these goals may be quite weak. In the latter, the choice of means tends to be dominated by norms of efficiency, and when the limiting case is reached, according to Merton (1957, p. 133), "any and all procedures which promise the attainment of the all-important goal would be permitted." Obviously, the limiting case is never reached. If it were, society as we know it would not exist. There would be no legitimate (or illegitimate) means and interaction would be characterized by a "war of all against all," which is the antithesis of society. But the concept of such a hypothetical limiting case is nevertheless useful for heuristic purposes. The way in which Merton uses it in his formulation of the theory of anomie will be discussed presently.

The above case is but one type of "malintegrated" society. At the other extreme is that type of society in which the emphasis on institutional means is so great that they tend to become ends-in-themselves. As such, they require no justification in utilitarian terms and conformity to them becomes "ritualistic." As might be expected, societies of this type tend to be highly stable and resistant to change, which in the short run may be quite functional. But in the long run, presumably, it is not, for there is too little flexibility to adapt to new life conditions. Between these extremes, says Merton (1957, p. 134):

> [A]re societies which maintain a rough balance between emphases upon cultural goals and institutionalized practices, and these constitute the integrated and relatively stable, though changing societies.

Of these two polar types of malintegrated societies, Merton is concerned primarily with the type which emphasizes cultural goals rather more than institutional means. His concern in this regard stems first from the fact that he is interested in the phenomenon of anomie (which he argues is likely to be great in societies of this type) and, second, from the fact that he is interested in contemporary American society (which he argues approximates this type).

Merton is concerned in his formulation of the theory of anomie with variations in rates of deviance *between* the polar types just described, as well as variation rates *within* the polar type represented by the American case. It will be argued here that a thorough understanding of his work requires the separation of these two aspects of his theory. This is not an easy task to accomplish, it might be noted, because Merton does not distinguish clearly between the two aspects of his theory. Moreover, it can be accomplished only by a process of abstraction, which carries with it the risk of distortion. But the task is an important one and, on balance, justified in spite of the attendant risks.

Merton's thesis on variations in rates of deviant behavior between the polar types described above has received relatively little attention from those who have dealt with his work. Nearly all of it has centered on his explanation for variations in rates of deviance within the polar type represented by the American case. Why this is so is an intriguing question in the sociology of knowledge, but one which is beyond the scope of the present discussion.[11] The substance of Merton's thesis is this: One can expect higher rates of deviance in societies of the American type, as compared with societies of the "ritualistic" type, because the relatively greater stress on goal-attainment in the former renders the norms prescribing legitimate means ineffective in controlling the use of technically more efficient ones. Merton (1957, p. 135) put it as follows:

> With such a differential emphasis on goals and institutional procedures, the latter may be so vitiated by the stress on goals as to have the behavior of individuals limited only by considerations of technical expediency. In this context, the sole significant question becomes: Which of the available procedures is most efficient in netting the culturally approved value? The technically most effective procedure, whether culturally legitimate or not, becomes typically preferred to institutionally prescribed conduct. As the process of attenuation continues, the society becomes unstable and there develops what Durkheim called "anomie" (or normlessness).

One implication of Merton's position seems clear: The greater the emphasis on goal-attainment in relation to the emphasis on institutional means, the greater will be the tendency for participants in such a system to engage in deviant forms of behavior. Thus, in the case where the emphasis on goal-attainment is greater than the emphasis on institutional means, deviance is a function of the disparity between the two emphases. It follows also that the disparity can increase as a result of an increase in the emphasis on cultural goals in relation to institutional means, or of a decrease in the emphasis on institutional means in relation to cultural goals, or of both.

Another implication, and one which will be stressed because

it is so often overlooked in evaluating Merton's thesis, is that societies of the American type, as compared with societies of the ritualistic type, are likely to have higher rates of deviance at all levels within the system, among the rich as well as the poor, among the powerful as well as the powerless, among those with high status as well as those with low status. On the assumption that Merton is correct in classifying American society as he does, his thesis should go a long way toward explaining the deviance in high places in America, e.g., among successful corporation executives, politicians in high office, and football coaches whose teams are ranked nationally.

It is this aspect of Merton's theory of anomie which relates most closely to the discussion of anomie by Durkheim in *The Division of Labor*. In that discussion, it will be recalled, anomie is a condition in which the relations of men in the market are unregulated because the norms necessary for their regulation have not yet developed. Merton, on the other hand, starts with the assumption that such norms are already in existence, but too weak to control the tendency toward the use of technically more efficient means which the emphasis on goal-attainment generates. Thus they are both talking about a situation in which the means which men use are unregulated. But there is a difference. With Durkheim the means are not in violation of established regulatory norms, whereas with Merton they are. This is why, given Merton's concept of anomie, it is quite appropriate to classify the resulting expediency as deviant behavior. In summary terms, then, the difference may be stated as follows: Expediency in the context of *The Division of Labor* is due to an undeveloped state of normative regulation, while in the context of Merton's thesis, it is due to the inability of established norms to keep it under control.[12]

It should be clear that the kind of deviance with which Merton is concerned is that which results from *participation in* a system of institutionalized goals and means. One would not expect the kind of pressure to commit deviant acts of which Merton speaks except among persons who aspire to attain the culturally favored goals. Moreover, it is clear that Merton is talking about *deviation from* a set of institutionalized cultural elements. Thus the deviant is not an "outsider" who happens to violate the norms of the system, but an "insider" who violates them because of problems associated with being a participant in that system. All this does not preclude the possibility that a deviant may become an outsider, in our view. Old commitments can be replaced by new ones. But when they are, the actor is technically no longer a deviating member of the old system but a conforming member of the new one. However, it is most important to understand that in such a case, the actor is a deviant *before* he becomes an outsider, not *because* he is an outsider, as some have argued (Cf. Becker, 1963).

In this connection, it is worthy of note that Merton considers it very unlikely that old commitments will be completely extinguished, even in those cases where the actor is thoroughly alienated and highly motivated to reject the cultural elements which are the objects of old commitments. In a very revealing footnote to his discussion of the consequences of withdrawing emotional support from institutional norms, Merton (1957, p. 136) makes the following statement:

> It appears unlikely that cultural norms, once interiorized, are wholly eliminated. Whatever residuum persists will induce personality tensions and conflict, with some measure of ambivalence. A manifest rejection of the once-incorporated institutional norms will be coupled with some latent retention of their emotional correlates. Guilt feelings, a sense of sin, pangs of conscience are diverse terms referring to this unrelieved tension.

Put another way, even when there is a manifest rejection of the troublesome cultural elements, the actor may possess a latent orientation to those very same elements. Moreover, this latent orientation may affect his behavior in such a way as to justify arguing he is "reacting against" the old cultural elements, even when he is conforming to new ones.

It seems appropriate at this time to comment further on the significance of the points just covered in relation to certain criticisms of the theory of anomie. It has been argued by Becker (1963) that deviants are "outsiders" who are deviant because of a process of labeling by "insiders" who are powerful enough to make those labels "stick." Presumably, such outsiders are not motivated by system-generated pressures to react against cultural elements to which they are committed, as anomie theorists contend. Rather, they are conforming to a system of cultural elements which for any number of reasons just happen to be different from those of the established system. Thus they are deviant only because they are labeled as such by representatives of the established system. In other words, deviance is a function of a process of labeling, not a process of disaffection and adaptation. Under the labeling perspective the outsider is no different psychologically from the insider. Both are conformists. The difference lies in the fact that the norms to which the outsider conforms are classified as deviant by the insider.

Anomie theorists, it should be noted, recognize the existence of deviant norms (e.g., those found in delinquent gangs) to which persons conform and, as a result, acquire the label of deviant. But they tend to see such norms as the result of a process of disaffection, adaptation and, in time, institutionalization. Once they are established, they stand as ready-made solutions to problems presented by the conventional normative system.[13] As such, they are attractive to those who possess the problem for which they are a solution. Anomie theorists therefore not only recognize the existence of deviant norms, but also have an explanation for their existence which is consistent with their overall theoretical perspective. This is not the case with labeling theorists. For the most part labeling theorists fail to deal with the question: why are the deviant norms there for persons to conform to?

Returning to the substance of Merton's thesis, it is, of course, an empirical question as to whether American society approximates the polar type in which the emphasis on goal-attainment so exceeds the emphasis on legitimate means as to make the control of expediency difficult. Merton's original paper proffers some support for his contention that it does, although his facts relate rather more to the emphasis in America on monetary success than to the de-emphasis on the use of legitimate means in achieving this success. Drawing from a variety of published works on the success theme in American society, he concludes the following (1957, pp. 136-139):

1. Although money is not the only success goal in America, it is an important one. This is true in part because of the function of money as a medium of exchange.
2. The source of one's money is a variable affecting one's status, but the anonymity of urban life makes it possible to translate money acquired by illegitimate means into high status—if not immediately, then "in the course of time."
3. The American Dream of monetary success is "indefinite and relative," i.e., no specific amount of money is designated as the amount one must acquire to be a success. As a result, no matter how much one acquires, there is almost always someone who had acquired more and who is therefore more successful. Thus with few exceptions we are all destined to be failures in relation to someone else.[14]
4. The goal of monetary success in America is accompanied by a number of ideological beliefs, which may be said to function to keep the motivation of the participants in the system high in relation to continued pursuit of that goal. Among the more important of these beliefs are the following: First, that the goal is available to all members of the society, regardless of birth; second, precisely because it is available to all, it is incumbent upon all to pursue it; and third, even in the face of repeated failure to reach the goal, all are duty bound to continue in its pursuit, i.e., one must not be a "quitter." In this connection, we are reminded that seeming failure is often only a way-station to eventual success and, further, that the cardinal sin in America is not failure to reach the goal, but failure to continue in one's efforts to do so.

The other aspect of Merton's theory—and the one which has received the most attention from American criminologists—has to do with rates of deviance *within* the polar type represented by the American case. If it may be said that the tendency toward deviance is generally great in societies which simultaneously emphasize the attainment of certain success goals and de-emphasize the norms prescribing legitimate means to those goals, then one would expect the tendency toward deviance to be even greater among those classes of persons whose access to the means which may legitimately be used is limited. This is the logic of Merton's explanation for the higher rates of deviance in the lower classes, for it is in these classes, obviously, that access to legitimate means is most severely limited. So that there will be no misunderstanding of what Merton is saying, it should be noted that it is not simply the existence of a class structure (which provides unequal access to legitimate means) that explains the higher rates of deviance in the lower classes, but the combination of such a class structure *plus* an emphasis on goal attainment which transcends class lines. Merton (1957, p. 146) put it this way:

> It is only when a system of cultural values extols, virtually above all else, certain *common* success-goals, *for the population at large*, while the social structure rigorously restricts or completely closes access to approved modes of reaching these goals *for a considerable part of the same population*, that deviant behavior ensues on a large scale.

One obvious conclusion which may be drawn from all this is that whether one is focusing on the deviance which results from the emphasis on goals over means or from the commitment of lower class persons to goals which are difficult to attain given their access to legitimate means, structural features of the social system which are considered "good" are responsible for conditions which are considered "bad." Merton saw this clearly and at one point argued (1957, p. 146), "a cardinal American virtue, 'ambition,' promotes a cardinal American vice, 'deviant behavior.'"

It should now be clear what Merton means by anomie. In the context of his theory of deviance, anomie is a state of social organization (or, if one prefers, disorganization) in which there is a rejection of prevailing cultural goals, or institutional means, or both or, as we suggest below, a tendency to do so that may be expressed in a variety of ways. Its sources are several, as we have seen, but in all cases it is the result of participation in an institutional system of cultural elements. The persons involved can thus be expected to be ambivalent because they are motivated to reject elements of the culture to which they are committed by virtue of their participation. It will be remembered that if the actor is not to some extent committed to certain institutional elements within the society in question, he will not have the problem for which rejection of one or more of these elements is a solution. It follows from all this that *the theory of anomie, as a theory of deviance, explains only those departures from the norms of an institutionalized system that result from participation in that system.* All other departures are beyond its scope of explanation.

In summary, Merton's reasoning with respect to the motivation involved in rule-violation in societies represented by the American case is as follows: First, socialization in societies of this type produces more concern with attaining the cultural goals than with conforming to the norms prescribing legitimate means. It follows that satisfactions will be derived more from winning than from sheer participating in competitive activity. Put another way, societies of this type generate such intense pressures to attain the cultural goals that the choice of means tends to be determined mainly by considerations of technical efficiency, with little regard for what is institutionally approved. This polar type tends to be quite unstable and exemplifies what Merton means by anomie (or normlessness). Second, socialization in societies of this type produces concern for attaining the cultural goals even among those whose access to the means which may legitimately be used is limited, that is, even within the lower classes. This leads to disaffection with institutional means, or with the goals, or both, and thus to deviant forms of behavior. In all cases these deviant forms of behavior may be seen as "individual adaptations" to system-generated pressures.

Modes of Individual Adaptation

Merton lists four types of such individual adaptations. It is important to understand that all four modes of individual adaptation refer to "ways of behaving" and not to "personality types."

A given individual may manifest two or more of these "ways" in relation to the pressures he faces. On the other hand, having said this does not preclude the possibility that a particular individual may respond rather consistently in a particular way to a wide range of pressures. That is, the behavior of an individual may become patterned and thus constitute a generalized tendency of the type referred to as a personality trait.

All types are considered deviant in that they involve behavior which departs in some sense from prevailing institutional arrangements. They are presented schematically in the following table, in which (+) stands for "acceptance," (–) stands for "rejection," and (–/+) stands for "rejection of prevailing institutional arrangements and substitution of alternatives ones."

	Institutional Means	Culturally Favored Goals
Innovation	–	+
Ritualism	+	–
Retreatism	–	+
Rebellion	–/+	–/+

Figure 1. Merton's Modes of Individual Adaptation (Adapted from Merton, 1957, p. 140).

Innovation as a mode of individual adaptation involves the use of illegitimate means in the pursuit of prevailing cultural goals. Often such means are more effective than legitimate ones—which helps explain their attractiveness—but, of course they need not be. Innovation occurs, as Figure 1 indicates, when there is continued acceptance of prevailing cultural goals in combination with rejection of the norms prescribing legitimate means to these goals. On the question of its distribution, Merton contends that it is likely to be found at all economic levels within a society such as our own (because of the stress at all levels on the attainment of cultural goals), but that the rates will be higher in the lower strata than in the higher strata (because of the relative lack of access in the lower strata to the means which may legitimately be used in pursuing the cultural goals).

Support for his contention that innovation is likely to be found at all levels within a society such as our own may be seen in the historical accounts of the Robber Barons, the studies of white collar crime, and the self-report studies of illegal activity among the more "respectable" people in our society. Merton cites a number of studies in support of his claim, but it should be noted that the evidence available to him in 1938 was far less than it is now. Subsequent research leaves little doubt that Merton was correct in his somewhat speculative conclusions on the subject.[15]

Support for the contention that innovation is likely to be greater in the lower class than in the higher classes may be seen in the official statistics of law enforcement agencies. This source of data has been called into question by a number of sociologists, on the grounds that there is a "class bias" in the way law enforcement agencies operate. Specifically, it has been argued that were it not for this bias the rates would be similar from one class to another. But it might be argued that only what is treated officially as crime is crime in any realistic conception of the term. That is to say, if some men are typically not treated as criminals when they commit acts that are defined as crime by statute, then it would be better from the point of view of understanding patterns of criminality to eliminate such acts from the category of crime, rather than to argue that much crime is overlooked by the class bias in law enforcement. This is another way of saying the anticipated official response to a given act should be an element in the definition of that act as crime or non-crime, regardless of whether, in some technical sense, it is against the law. Cloward and Ohlin (1960, pp. 6-7), commenting on this very point, argue as follows concerning the definition of delinquency:

> Acts that do not ordinarily lead to the initiation of delinquency proceedings may constitute deviance from the norms of some group or organization, such as church, school, social agency, family and peer groups; but these acts are not [i.e., should not be treated] delinquent unless they are likely to be defined as such by agents of criminal justice.

Their argument in support of an "official" definition of delinquency is simply this: An act which is perhaps frowned upon, but otherwise ignored by the officials of the criminal justice system, will not have the same meaning to the actor, and very likely to the community as well, as one which would ordinarily result in a charge of delinquency. The same logic, obviously, could be applied to crime. Thus, for sociological purposes, a meaningful definition of crime is "what is treated as crime by the officials of the system," and for sociological research on the subject, official statistics therefore may be quite appropriate.

Having made a case for the acceptance of an "official" definition of crime as the most meaningful one for socio-logical purposes, we should not conclude that "legal" definitions of crime (what is defined as crime by statute) are of no value whatsoever. In certain kinds of ideological disputes, for example, it might be quite useful to start with a "legal" definition of crime. Recent efforts to secure more rigorous enforcement of the laws pertaining to "white-collar crime" have done this. Arguments in this regard often take the following form: Although there is a great deal of white-collar crime being committed, very little of it is being prosecuted, because of a bias in law enforcement; furthermore, this kind of bias in the enforcement of law should be corrected, in all fairness to other classes of persons now being treated harshly by the law. But, however useful for ideological purposes a legal definition of crime may be, it is not useful for sociological purposes, if one is interested in crime as a category of deviant behavior.

Merton's analysis of innovation helps explain the facts available to us concerning the relationship between poverty and crime. It is well known that in America, and in many other societies as well, the two are highly correlated, especially if one is focusing on property crime. It is also well known that in some societies, poverty is not highly correlated with crime. Even when it is found "in the midst of plenty," poverty is not always correlated with crime. Poverty is most likely to be associated with crime when, as already suggested, the symbols of success are the same for those who are in the poverty classes as for those who are not. Merton (1957, p. 147) argues that the relatively low rates of crime in southeastern Europe may well be a function of the fact that in this area of Europe the "rigid class structure is coupled with *differential class symbols of success.*"

One obvious implication of Merton's thesis, in fact, of anomie theory in general, is that the relatively high rates of deviance in the lower classes (as a result of the combination of a cultural emphasis on success and limited access to the means by which success is achieved) could be significantly reduced (in those classes) either by de-emphasizing success or by providing greater access to the means by which success is achieved, or by some combination of the two. Put another way, a reduction in anomie from this source thus can be accomplished by bringing into alignment what people want and the means for getting what they want.

It is well to keep in mind that not all innovation, however deviant it may be from the point of view of the norms prescribing legitimate means, qualifies as crime. Crime is a legal concept and covers only those acts that are in violation of the law. Moreover, not all crime qualifies as innovation. Crimes of violence, for example, do not qualify as innovation unless they are committed in connection with the attainment of culturally-approved goals. Even some property crime does not qualify as innovation. This is true, for example, of much vandalism, which seems to be an end-in-itself rather than a means to an end, especially if by "end" we mean one which is culturally approved. As will be seen, the fact that much delinquency does not qualify as innovation is the primary basis for a major qualification of Merton's version of the theory of anomie introduced some years later by Albert K. Cohen (1955) and treated below.

The second of the modes of "individual adaptation" is ritualism. According to Merton (1957, pp. 149-50):

> It involves the abandoning or scaling down of the lofty cultural goals of great pecuniary success and rapid social mobility to the point where one's aspirations can be satisfied. But though one rejects the cultural obligation to attempt "to get ahead in the world," though one draws in one's horizons, one continues to abide almost compulsively by institutional norms.

Ritualism, like innovation, is related inversely to social class, but it is most likely to be found among those lower-middle-class persons who are having difficulty attaining the culturally favored goals legitimately, but who are too committed to the norms prescribing legitimate means to use illegitimate ones. The compulsive quality of the adherence to institutional norms suggests a kind of reaction formation, so that conformity is not without ambivalence, but it is conformity nevertheless, and so the pattern can be considered deviant only in so far as it involves rejection of the obligation to continue striving for lofty goals.[16] Since the penalty for rejection of this obligation is not usually very great, ritualism as a solution is probably the most common of those treated in the scheme and the preferred adaptation among lower-middle-class persons. For Merton, ritualism can be expected in the lower middle class because it is here that deep commitments to the institutional norms are likely to develop. In Merton's own words on the subject (1957, p. 151):

> It is in the lower middle class that parents typically exert continuous pressure upon children to abide by the moral mandates of the society, and where the social climb upward is less likely to meet with success than among the upper middle class. The strong disciplining for conformity with mores reduces the likelihood of innovation and promotes the likelihood of ritualism.

The third of the modes of "individual adaptation" discussed by Merton is retreatism. It involves the rejection of both cultural goals and institutional means. In this category, Merton (1957, p. 153) classifies the activities of "psychotics, artists, pariahs, outcasts, vagrants, vagabonds, tramps, chronic drunkards, and drug addicts" in so far as they manifest the pattern of rejection described. Sociologically, retreatists are the true aliens and may be seen as being "*in* the society but not *of* it" (Merton, 1957, p. 157). This does not mean that their activities are not the result of participation in the society, or that their activities are not problematic for the society and likely to be classified as deviant, but only that in "not sharing the common frame of values, they can be included as members of the *society* (in distinction from the *population*) only in a fictional *sense*" (Merton, 1957, p. 153). Nor does their status as aliens mean that all traces of commitment to the institutionalized cultural elements have been eliminated in the process of rejecting them. As mentioned earlier, Merton recognizes that it is difficult to completely eliminate all traces of commitment to such cultural elements once they have been "interiorized," which means that persons who choose to retreat may still face internal "strains" leading to feelings of guilt or doubt and the various defense mechanisms associated with such feelings.

The last of the four deviant modes of individual adaptation is called rebellion. Like retreatism, it involves a rejection of the cultural goals and institutional means, but, unlike retreatism, it involves an attempt to replace them with acceptable alternatives. Persons involved in a pattern of rebellion have a "cause" for which they are fighting. Because of this fact the pattern is often a collective one, for there are obvious advantages in collective action when social change is the objective. Concerning the distribution of rebellion, Merton has little to say, except to point out that "it is typically members of the rising class rather than the most depressed strata who organize the resentful and the rebellious into a revolutionary group" (1957, p. 157).

It is important to note that in the discussion of rebellion, Merton specifically excludes a category of behavior that could be traced to the disparity between goals and means with which he is concerned in his treatment of variations within societies of the American type. Referred to by the term *ressentiment*, it is a pattern of behavior in which the actor retains some considerable commitment to the objects of value against which he is rebelling. Thus, it is behavior in which the actor condemns what he secretly craves. He in effect solves his problem by a process of rationalization in which he argues that the goal is not worth having. Rebellion, on the other hand, is a type of behavior in which the actor has extinguished whatever commitments he may have had to the objects of value against which he is rebelling. Rebellion, for Merton (1957, p. 156) "involves a genuine transvaluation, where the direct or vicarious experience of frustration leads to full denunciation of previously prized values."[17]

It may be assumed that Merton recognized that *ressentiment* could be traced to the disparity between goals and means, but felt either that it was an insignificant category or that it was significant, but did not fit neatly into his analytic scheme. Whatever his assumptions in this regard, he recognized that some individuals who condemn established goals and means do so before they have extinguished their commitments to those goals and means, leaving them ambivalent and inclined to react in the manner described. Later we shall see that it is precisely the type of response Merton called *ressentiment* which became, for Cohen, the one which best describes the motivation of the gang delinquent.[18]

Earlier it was noted that Merton's thesis with respect to variations between the polar types treated in his 1938 paper has been largely ignored by American sociologists. In this connection, it is interesting to note that at least one critic goes further and specifically denies that Merton concerns himself with the consequences of self-interested striving (egoism, in Durkheim's terms) for expediency on the level of means in societies of the American type. Reference is to the words of Horton (1964, pp. 294-95):

> Merton's anomie differs from that of Durkheim in one crucial respect—in its identification with the very groups and values which Durkheim saw as the prime source of anomie in industrial societies. For Durkheim, anomie was endemic in such societies not only because of inequality in the conditions of competition, but more importantly, because self-interested striving (for status and success goals) had been raised to social ends. The institutionalization of self-interest meant the legitimization of anarchy and amorality. Morality requires, according to Durkheim . . . social goals obeyed out of disinterest and altruism, not self-interest and egoism. To maximize opportunities for achieving success would in no way end anomie.

In the judgment of this writer, Horton is clearly wrong. One can only conclude that Horton, like so many others, has failed to read Merton carefully. Merton, as indicated above, discusses two sources of anomie, one of which is precisely the source which Horton claims Merton failed to recognize.

In summary, then, Merton's theory of anomie is an attempt to explain variations in rates of deviance *between* societies of the American type and so-called "ritualistic" societies, as well as variations in rates of deviance *within* societies of the American type. As such, it involves two related sources of anomie: The emphasis on goals (as compared with institutionally approved means), and the relative lack of opportunity in the lower classes. Concerning the first of these sources, anomie results when institutions are unable to control the tendency toward expediency in the choice of means that is produced by the emphasis on cultural goals. Concerning the second of these sources, anomie results when persons in the lower strata come to realize the difficulties they face in attaining the approved goals by legitimate means and proceed to reject the approved goals, the institutional means, or both. The two sources are similar in that both involve a heavy emphasis on goal-attainment. What differentiates them is the fact that in the latter there is a recognition of the differences by class in access to the means which may legitimately be used in attaining the approved goals.

By recognizing both aspects of Merton's theory, it is possible to point up the continuity between Durkheim and Merton. *What Merton means by an emphasis on goals as compared with institutional means is what Durkheim meant by the egoistic tendencies in individualism.* The fact that Merton saw anomie as resulting also from inequality of opportunity in combination with an emphasis on common success goals in no way denies this continuity, Horton's statement to this effect notwithstanding.

On the other hand, Merton's reformulation of the theory of anomie does involve one very important difference from the position taken by Durkheim. The tendency to aspire to higher and higher levels of goals is not, as in Durkheim's version of the theory, a natural one that societies sometimes fail to regulate. Rather, it is culturally induced. Thus Merton breaks with the nineteenth century tradition, which sees unsocialized men as having insatiable desires for money, power, and status, and the creature comforts that they afford. The difference between Merton and Durkheim in this regard may seem inconsequential, since the result in both cases is that men desire more than they can realistically expect to get, under existing institutional arrangements. But in terms of the implications for change, the differences are far from inconsequential. If men do not naturally possess a tendency to aspire to higher and higher levels of goals, the presence of unrealistic aspirations is not a problem in the area of social control but a problem in the area of socialization. The "solution" implied in Merton's formulation of the theory of anomie, other things being equal, is not more control over appetites, but less emphasis on goal-attainment in the process of socialization. Put another way, for Merton, if men are ambitious, it is because the system requires it, and if their ambition motivates them to want what by legitimate means is difficult to attain, society, not the individual, is responsible. The basis for our judgment that Merton was a radical social critic should now be evident.

Our aim has been to expose the more important aspects of Merton's theory of anomie and to spell out some of the implication for understanding deviance generally, but particularly in America. We have also pointed out some of the shortcomings in Merton's formulation of the theory and some of the issues he left unresolved. As a kind of preface to dealing with various efforts with respect to the further development of the theory, it might be useful to list the more important of these shortcomings and unresolved issues, because, for the most part, they have become the focus of attention of those efforts.

One obvious shortcoming has to do with the question of the extent of the ambivalence present in those who have adapted to their circumstances through one or more of the modes of individual adaptation to which Merton calls our attention. True, he recognizes the likelihood of ambivalence among those who have "interiorized" the cultural elements which they later reject, and the possibility that this ambivalence may then lead to various defense mechanisms as ways of managing it, but he does not deal extensively with the subject. In fact, he almost ignores it.

As we shall see, this is an area in which Talcott Parsons makes a significant contribution.

A related shortcoming in Merton's formulation of the theory has to do with the status of *ressentiment* as a reaction to the perceived inability to reach one's goals by legitimate means. For reasons which are not apparent from a reading of his work, Merton has chosen not to include it within his scheme. He argues it should not be confused with rebellion, the only category into which it might logically be placed, depending of course on how broadly the category is defined. The fact that it is not covered by his scheme would be of little consequence if it could be shown that only a small percentage of all deviance is characterized by the kind of reaction which is involved. But a number of theorists have argued that the percentage of deviant acts which may be so characterized is quite large. Thus to ignore *ressentiment* is to ignore an important category of deviance. Albert K. Cohen's theory of gang delinquency (treated below) includes the argument that much of what gang delinquents do is best explained by reference to the kind of ambivalence and subsequent reaction which is implied in *ressentiment*.

Another shortcoming of Merton's formulation of the theory has to do with the extent to which his "adaptations" become institutionalized, as ready-made solutions, for example, to certain problems of adjustment within the lower classes in America. Although much of what Merton says is not inconsistent with the idea that institutionalization of his adaptations may be quite common, he does not specifically deal with the subject. Cohen, on the other hand, does. We shall call attention to Cohen's ideas in this regard as we expose his theory of gang delinquency.

Still another shortcoming in Merton's formulation has to do with the role of social structure in determining the types of deviant adaptations which various categories of persons may choose in solving their problems. Merton places almost exclusive stress on factors internal to the actor in his discussion of how system-generated problems are solved. Cloward and Ohlin, on the other hand, stress structural features of the situation in which actors (individually or collectively) find themselves. The ideas of Cloward and Ohlin in this regard will be dealt with below.

Perhaps the most important shortcoming of Merton's theory of anomie has to do, on the one hand, with the question of the functional significance (for industrial societies) of common success goals and, on the other, with the source of the inequality of opportunity which plays such an important part in his thinking about differences in rates of deviance within societies of the American type. Ideas on both these subjects have been developed at length by sociologists, but have not been related to the theory of anomie in any systematic way. Thus, the full impact of these ideas is often missed by those who use them in their theories of deviance. Put another way, unless one understands what lies behind the common success goals and the inequality of opportunity in modern industrial societies, one can hardly be expected to appreciate the magnitude of the problem faced by those who may want to deal constructively with anomie and its consequences in human society.

Extensions and Reformulations

The task in the following sections is to expose certain contributions to the theory of anomie of Talcott Parsons, Albert K. Cohen, and two men who published together, Richard Cloward and Lloyd Ohlin. The emphasis will be on those contributions which have resulted in significant advances in our understanding of deviance in America.

Talcott Parsons and the Theory of Deviance

To be considered first is Talcott Parsons' views on the genesis and direction of deviant motivation. The most elaborate statement of his views on the subject appeared in *The Social System* (1951). In that statement, Parsons was concerned with deviance in general, so that what is here conceived as a contribution to the theory of anomie may well have been inadvertent (from the point of view of his motivation for making it). His discussion of the genesis and direction of deviant motivation, as will be obvious, involves more psychology than much of what passes for sociology in America, because, for Parsons, no matter how much of the actor's motivation may be explained by reference to the experiences he may have had as a member of various groups within the society, the motivation itself is an individual phenomenon. For Parsons, there is no such thing as group motivation. His discussion of the genesis of deviant motivation deals with how the motivation to engage in acts defined as deviant is built up. His discussion of the directions of deviant motivation deals with the ways in which that motivation becomes differentiated and, to some extent, why.

Throughout his discussion of both subjects, Parsons makes sharp analytic distinctions between *socialization*, *deviance*, and *social control*. He defines *socialization* as a process by which the cultural elements of the society (or any of its component parts) are transmitted. From the point of view of the actor, it is the process by which the actor acquires those cultural elements, including, in many cases, commitments to them. *Deviance* may be defined in two ways, depending upon whether the point of reference is the individual actor or the interactive system. In the first context, says Parsons (1951, p. 250) deviance is a "motivated tendency for an actor to behave in contravention of one or more institutionalized normative patterns," while in the second, it is a "tendency on the part of one or more of the component actors to behave in such a way as to disturb the equilibrium of the interactive process." In both contexts, deviance is defined in relation to the institutionalized norms of an interactive system. Moreover, and most important, as we shall see, the actor is motivated to contravene the norms of the system in which he is a participant. Thus with Parsons, as with Merton, the deviant is a member of the group whose norms he violates. In the terms used earlier, he is an "insider" not an "outsider."

Social control is defined as those motivated processes within the actor or among those with whom he is in interaction by which deviance is, or tends to be, counteracted. As not all attempts at counteraction succeed, deviance may be seen as resulting either in successful counteraction or in change in the structure of the interactive system.

For those who are not familiar with the orientation of modern sociology, it might be useful to note that conformity to established norms is not considered "good" in a moral sense any more than deviance is considered "bad." Questions of morality are outside the frame of reference of science, which has become the prevailing method by which modern sociology has attempted to understand its subject matter.

Parsons begins his discussion of the genesis of deviant motivation by reference to a hypothetical stable interactive system. In such a system the participants are interacting in terms of a normative pattern which they share and have internalized. They are, moreover, sufficiently attached to one another to be sensitive to each other's reactions to any violations of that normative pattern. Parsons then posits the introduction of a disturbance "from whatever source," creating a strain to the relationship. For example, "A" may fail to live up to the expectations of "B," presenting both with a "problem of adjustment." To simplify matters, we shall focus on the problem faced by "B" in attempting to adjust to the changed behavior of "A." On the most general level of analysis, there are a limited number of ways in which "B" can solve his problem, says Parsons (1951, p. 252):

> He can first restructure his own need-dispositions, by inhibition and by one or more of the mechanisms of defense, such as simply repressing the needs which are no longer gratified. He can, secondly, seek to transfer his cathexis to a new object and relieve the strain that way and, finally, he can renounce or seek to redefine the value orientation pattern with which alter [in our terms, "A"] is conforming.

Should "B" successfully move in any one of these three directions, the strain in the relationship would be resolved. It would be resolved also if "A" were to abandon his changed behavior. It should be apparent that resolution in the first case (through a process of learning by "B") would result in a changed state of the interactive system, in the second (through "A" abandoning his changed behavior) a restoration of the old state.

There is another possible outcome, says Parsons, and one which is quite likely, because of the difficulty in making changes when one is a committed participant in the interactive system. That is, in one or more of the areas of possible change, a "compromise" solution may be reached. To take one example, "B" may not be able to "transfer his cathexis to a new object" because of the strength of his attachment to "A." But where this is the case, the relationship can no longer continue undisturbed. As Parsons (1951, p. 253) puts it:

> Ego ["B" in our example] must have some reaction to the frustration which alter ["A" in our example] has imposed upon him, some resentment or hostility. In other words the [attachment] acquires an ambivalent character; there is still the need to love or admire alter, but there is also the product of his frustration in the form of negative and in some sense hostile attitudes toward alter.

It is of course possible, says Parsons, for the negative or hostile attitudes to be directed, not toward the person or persons involved, but toward the normative pattern in terms of which the problematic expectations derive. In this case the resulting ambivalence would take the form of simultaneous positive and negative attitudes toward the same normative pattern.

The adaptations to which Merton points as at least partial solutions to the "problems of adjustment" presented to its members by societies of the American type, may be seen as more specific examples of the general solutions referred to by Parsons in his discussion of the directions of deviant motivation. Parsons (1951, p. 257-59) makes this very point in his discussion of the genesis and directions of deviant motivation. But most important for present purposes is to recognize that both Merton and Parsons note the likelihood of ambivalence in the personalities of those who adapt by one or more of the modes covered by their analyses. Moreover, both feel that the greater the degree of internalization of elements of the shared normative system, the greater the likelihood of ambivalence, whatever the solution attempted.

Thus nothing in the above analysis of Parsons' views on the genesis of deviant motivation is inconsistent in any fundamental way with what Merton had to say in his original paper. However, in concerning himself with the psycho-dynamics of the genesis of deviant motivation, Parsons provides us with additional insight into the significance of commitment both to persons and to normative elements in the development of the negative component of ambivalence. Moreover, his concerns in this regard have led to important conclusions about the *extent* of ambivalence among these same persons. For Parsons it is far greater than has been suggested by Merton, and, as we shall see, far more important in explaining subsequent responses.

Parsons' discussion of the directions of deviant motivation builds directly on his discussion of the genesis of deviant motivation. He argues that while there are many ways in which the strains inherent in an ambivalent motivational structure may be handled, they all fall into one of two general categories. The first involves repression of one side of the ambivalent motivational structure so as to permit a relatively undisturbed expression of the other side. The second involves an attempt to gratify both sides of the ambivalent motivational structure. Presumably the latter cannot be accomplished within the same concrete situation, because the two sides are in conflict. But in a complex society such as our own, there are all sorts of possibilities to gratify both sides, for example, by segregating contexts and occasions.

In discussing the directions of deviant motivation, Parsons concentrates on the first of these approaches. He begins by noting that although one side of the ambivalent motivation structure is repressed, this does not mean that it is of no consequence in explaining what the actor does. In fact, the repressed component figures prominently in Parsons' explanation of probable responses to ambivalence. But before taking on that aspect of Parsons' treatment of the subject, it is necessary to define certain terms. Parsons refers to the negative component of the actor's ambivalent motivational structure as the *alienative* component, and to the positive component as the *conformative* component. When the *alienative* component is dominant, he speaks of an *alienative dominance* in the actor's need-disposition structure. When the *conformative* component is dominant, he speaks of a *conformative dominance* in the actor's need-disposition structure.

Depending upon which of the two components is dominant, Parsons speaks of a tendency toward *compulsive alienation* or *compulsive conformity*. His reasons for suggesting a tendency toward compulsion in responding to an alienative or a conformative dominance are simple and, it might be added, fundamental to much of his thinking on the subject of deviant motivation. What he argues is that no matter which of the two components is dominant, the actor has a problem of managing the one that is repressed. He must keep it under control, so to speak, or it will break through and present additional problems of adjustment. One important mechanism of defense against the repressed component breaking through is *reaction formation*. The overt manifestation of reaction formation is an exaggerated expression of the dominant side of the ambivalent motivational structure. The tendency in the case of compulsive conformity is to "accentuate the positive," to be "compulsively careful" to conform to institutionalized expectations. In the case of compulsive alienation, the tendency is to "accentuate the negative," to be "compulsively careful" *not* to conform to the institutionalized expectations.

Parsons does not stop here in his effort to differentiate motivations arising out of ambivalence. Compulsive conformity and compulsive alienation are further differentiated by a variable, well-known to psychologists, that having to do with more or less control over the situation than one would normally expect. Referred to by Parsons as the activity-passivity dimension, it is combined with compulsive conformity and compulsive alienation to produce four types of deviant motivation: A tendency toward compulsive performance, a tendency toward compulsive acquiescence, a tendency toward rebelliousness, and a tendency toward withdrawal. The four types of deviant motivation and the combinations of variables which give rise to them may be seen in Figure 2. By motivation, in this context, is meant simply a tendency or disposition to act in a certain way. It is important, according to Parsons, to separate deviant motivation from deviant behavior, because the former is not always expressed and the latter cannot be adequately explained without some reference to the situation in which the person who presumably possesses deviant tendencies finds himself. It might be noted in passing that much early psychology failed to take this important distinction into account, and thus attempted to explain deviance in terms of motivational patterns alone.

	Activity	*Passivity*
Conformative Dominance	Tendency Toward Compulsive Performance	Tendency Toward Compulsive Acquiescence
Alienative Dominance	Tendency Toward Rebelliousness	Tendency Toward Withdrawal

Figure 2. Types of Motivation (Adapted from Parsons, 1951, p. 257)

Inspection of Figure 2 will reveal that there are a number of similarities between Parsons' four types of deviant motivation and Merton's four modes of individual adaptation discussed above in Figure 1. Merton's "retreatism" is similar to Parsons' "tendency toward withdrawal," and Merton's "rebellion" is similar to Parsons' "tendency toward rebellion." Merton's "innovation" and his "ritualism" are more difficult to relate to Parsons' scheme, because they involve elements of conformative as well as alienative motivation, depending on whether one focuses on cultural goals or institutional means. In dealing with these similarities, it is important to keep in mind that while Merton was talking about types of deviant behavior, Parsons is talking about types of deviant motivation. The two typologies could be "brought together," so to speak, if one were willing to assume that Parsons' scheme applies to behavior as well as motivation, and, further, if one were to assume that each of Parsons' categories could apply to "cultural goals" as well as "institutional means." We have attempted to do this in Figure 3 below.

The value of Parsons' typology lies mainly in the fact that it calls attention to the variables which combine to produce each of the four categories of deviant motivation. The tendency toward withdrawal, for example, is a combination of an alienative dominance (in the actor's ambivalent motivational structure) plus a tendency toward passivity, while the tendency toward rebellion is a combination of an alienative dominance plus a tendency toward activity. Put this way, it can be seen that the tendency toward withdrawal and that toward rebellion are differentiated, not by any difference in the strength of the alienative component in relation to the conformative component—for in both cases they are the same—but by a difference on the activity-passivity dimension. If this seems inconsequential, consider this: For Parsons the motivation for much criminal activity is the tendency toward rebellion, while the motivation for much mental illness is the tendency toward withdrawal. If he is correct, then the difference between the criminal and a person who is mentally ill is less a matter of alienation than it is of a tendency toward activity or passivity. What this means, when one starts thinking about solutions to the problem of crime, is that in deterring a person from committing a criminal act we may be inducing him not to conform to conventional norms but to withdraw into the sick role or some other state of dependency. For many observers, withdrawal of this sort may be considered a desirable alternative, but it is not a solution to the problem of deviance, only to the problem of crime. Parsons pays a great deal of attention to the functional significance of the sick role. For example, the existence of a sick role, into which alienated people can withdraw, functions to "drain off" a great deal of alienative motivation that might otherwise be expressed in quite damaging ways—for example, in the form of personal and property crime. In making this point he concludes that there is much too little understanding of the sick role as a mechanism for "capturing" certain types of alienated people and for putting them into a position where they can do very little damage and are obligated by virtue of the norms involved, to try to get well, to get back into their normal social roles. Thus, he concludes further, that the system of medical practice performs important social control functions in so far as it deals with the alienative component of the motivational structure of those who withdraw into the sick role as a solution to their problems.

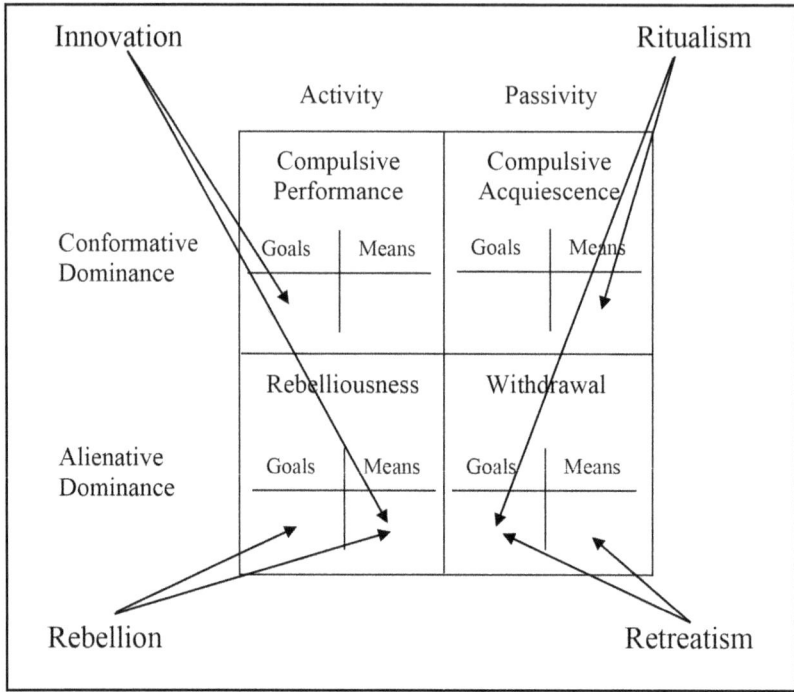

Figure 3. Relationship of Merton's Modes of Individual Adaptation to Parsons' Directions of Deviant Motivation

A similar analysis can be made of the differences between the tendency toward withdrawal, on the one hand, and that toward compulsive acquiescence, on the other. The difference lies not in the degree of emphasis on passivity—it is great in both cases—but in the fact that the former involves a dominance in the actor's motivational structure on the alienative side, while the latter involves a dominance on the conformative side. Thus a tendency toward withdrawal can be turned into a tendency toward compulsive acquiescence by decreasing the strength of the alienative component to a point where it is no longer dominant. The reverse is also true; a tendency toward compulsive acquiescence can be turned into a tendency toward withdrawal by increasing the strength of the alienative component.

Albert K. Cohen and Delinquent Subcultures

The work of Albert K. Cohen has been interpreted to be a rejection of Merton's formulation of the theory of anomie.[19] While it is true that Cohen calls attention to a number of shortcomings in the work of Merton, his criticisms are best seen as suggestions for revisions of the theory rather than a rejection of the theory itself. Moreover, there are several respects in which Cohen's work falls directly within the mainstream of thinking among anomie theorists. First, it is an attempt to explain differences in rates of behavior by reference to structural features of the larger society. Second, the features with which he is concerned are basically the same ones which attracted the attention of Durkheim and Merton, namely, the emphasis in modern societies on common success goals and the disadvantages associated with lower class status.

Cohen's contributions to the development of the theory of anomie are to be found mainly in his treatment of the phenomenon of gang delinquency. They appeared for the first time in 1955 in a work entitled *Delinquent Boys: the Culture of the Gang*.[20] As the title suggests, the focus of attention is on the subculture around which the gang is organized. The theory which he develops relates mainly to that subculture. For Cohen an "adequate" theory of gang delinquency must explain at least the following: First, the content of the subculture (Why does it have the peculiar configuration of traits which it has?), and second, the distribution of the subculture within the society at large (Why is it found primarily among certain categories of persons and not others?). There are other questions as well, which Cohen considers important and which he attempts to answer, but those concerning the content of the subculture and its distribution are the ones to which he gives the most attention.

It might be worth noting at this juncture in our treatment of the development of the theory of anomie generally that certain of the conclusions reached by Cohen are "culture bound," that is, are based upon an understanding of American society as it was structured at the time the study was done. For example, sex role changes that occurred in the period between 1955 and the present could not have been known and, obviously, were not taken into account. On the other hand, his approach to the theoretical questions involved is worthy of serious consideration, nevertheless, as we shall see.

The delinquent subculture is described in terms of six general characteristics. Five have to do specifically with its content. The sixth has to do with the quality of the attachment of its members to the gang. The first of the characteristics is a tendency for gang members to prefer non-utilitarian activities over utilitarian ones. By non-utilitarian activities is meant, simply, activities that one values as ends-in-themselves, rather than as means to (culturally-approved) ends. Much vandalism and violent behavior is seen by Cohen as non-utilitarian. Even the pattern of stealing seems often to have a non-utilitarian quality to it, when the items stolen are discarded or given away, and those that are not, have value in part because they were stolen. "The stolen sweets are often sweeter than those acquired by more legitimate and prosaic means" (Cohen, 1955, p. 26). The second of the characteristics is the subculture's negativism. He argues that what is right by delinquent norms is defined by its negative polarity to conventional norms. Delinquent gang behavior is considered right, says Cohen (1955, p. 28), "precisely because it is wrong by the norms of the larger culture." The third of the characteristic considered by Cohen is its maliciousness. In whatever they do "there is a kind of *malice* apparent, an enjoyment in the discomfiture of others, a delight in the defiance of the taboo itself" (Cohen, 1955, p. 27).

The fourth, fifth, and sixth characteristics are a tendency toward short-run hedonism, an emphasis on versatility, and group autonomy. By "short-run hedonism" is meant a tendency toward immediate gratification. Cohen notes that a pattern of immediate gratification is common throughout the lower classes, but argues that it comes to "full bloom" in the delinquent gang. Under this pattern there is little concern for planning, for the long-run consequences of present acts—in a word, for the future. The tendency is to live in the present and let the future take care of itself. By "versatility" Cohen means simply a tendency to avoid specialization, that is, to engage in a wide variety of activities. Lastly, by "group autonomy" is meant a tendency to resist being influenced by various agencies of control—the family, the church, social work agencies, etc.—which often function to regulate activities within the gang. As suggested earlier, Cohen is talking here not about the content of the subculture, but its attractiveness to the gang in relation to alternative ways of thinking and acting.

Concerning the distribution of the culture of the gang, Cohen contends that the pattern, as described, is found primarily among lower-class adolescent males. His thesis, as noted above, is an attempt to explain its distribution. In the simplest possible terms, the delinquent subculture is distributed the way it is because it is an attractive solution to a "problem of adjustment" found among this category of persons.

With respect to the nature of the problem, it is primarily one of social status (or lack thereof), of not being able to compete successfully with middle-class boys. Like their middle-class counterparts, lower-class boys are interested in success in school and on the job; however, unlike their middle-class counterparts, they lack the ability to measure up to the standards by which success in this area of activity is measured. The ability to which Cohen refers is a product of the pattern of socialization in the middle class. It includes such things as ambition, good manners, industry, thrift, the ability to defer immediate gratification, etc., none of which is likely to be as highly developed in the lower as in the middle class.

The problem would not be at all serious, says Cohen, if lower class boys did not care about the "good opinion" of those middle class persons with whom they interact, (e.g., their teachers in school), or if they did not to some extent internalize the standards by which success within the middle class is measured. But they do, and so it is serious. Cohen, (1955, p. 119) summarizes his position as follows:

> It may confidently be said that the *[lower class]* boy, particularly if his training and values be those we have here defined as working-class, is more likely than his middle-class peers to find himself at the bottom of the status hierarchy whenever he moves in a middle-class world, whether it be of adults or of children. To the degree to which he values middle-class status, either because he values the good opinion of middle-class persons or because he has to some degree internalized middle-class standards himself, he faces a problem of adjustment and is in the market for a solution.

In sum, the problem of adjustment of the lower-class adolescent male is primarily a problem of social status, that is, of ending up in the "loser" category whenever he competes with his middle-class counterparts in situations involving middle-class standards of success. And, to the extent that he internalizes these standards, he also faces a problem of self-esteem. The latter is a more serious problem in the sense that one cannot easily escape from it, for example, by withdrawing into a predominantly lower-class world. And being internal to the actor, the problem of self-esteem goes with him and can be solved only through a process of relearning, which is difficult to effect.

Cohen is not arguing that all lower-class adolescent males have internalized the middle-class standards by which success is measured. Nor is he arguing that all who have internalized these standards have done so to the same extent, but only that some have done so to some extent, and to the extent that they have, they are faced with a problem of self-esteem, as well as one of social status. Cohen then proceeds to point out that depending upon the extent of the problem he faces, the lower-class adolescent male is likely to end up alienated from the very standards he has internalized. As might be expected, this ambivalence can result in a compulsive rejection of the positive component of his ambivalence, the middle-class standards of success (an example of "reaction formation" as described by Parsons in his general theory of deviance), but not always, as we shall see. It is important to note that his conclusions are all very tentative and involve a great many deductions, but that is how theories are built, and Cohen is confident enough about his approach to the subject matter not to be deterred from presenting his views by the possibility of being wrong.

Cohen recognizes that, depending upon the situation of the lower-class boy, the ambivalence to which he refers may lead not to gang delinquency, but to a pattern of compulsive striving to escape from one's lower-class position. The compulsive striving, of course, is also explained in terms of the concept of reaction formation. He refers to this pattern as the "college boy" response and argues that a certain number of lower-class youth can be expected to respond in this way. However, because of the difficulties involved in this pattern, those who do are not likely to succeed unless possessed of unusual talent and/or motivation.

Finally, ambivalence may lead also to what Cohen refers to as the "stable corner boy" response. This response involves a passive acceptance of one's fate, based often on the belief that the future is not likely to be propitious. It is one that does not resolve the strains associated with failure, but then it does not involve the risks associated with being a delinquent either. A further discussion of the psychodynamics of the "college boy" and "corner boy" responses need not concern us here, except to note that they are treated by Cohen as alternative solutions to the problem of adjustment found among this category of males.

Two more points need to be mentioned: (1) Cohen reminds us that the delinquent sub-culture includes a set of standards which are the antithesis of those found in the middle classes. Thus the delinquent subculture is attractive in two respects: it expresses the lower-class male's negative feelings toward middle-class standards of success, and it provides him with a set of standards in terms of which he can succeed and (2) it is found more among males than females, because it is the male in our society who is under pressure to compete for status within the larger society.

It should be obvious that the thesis Cohen develops is tied to a period in our society in which sex roles were more differentiated than they subsequently came to be. Thus there is every reason to believe that as females in our society come to behave more like males, they will face similar problems of adjustment and react in similar ways. Indeed, the dramatic increase in the arrest rates for females in recent years may be interpreted as a function of sex-role changes and the problems of adjustment which such changes present.

It should be obvious also that the pattern of the delinquent which Cohen describes quite clearly does not fit into Merton's typology of deviant modes of individual adaptation. However, this should not be interpreted to mean, as some have argued (e.g., Clinard, 1964, pp. 30-33), that Cohen rejects the theory of anomie in its totality, for clearly he does not. All he says is that the "illicit means" thesis suggested by Merton as an explanation for much adult criminality does not explain the non-utilitarian emphasis within the delinquent subculture. In his own words (1955, p. 36):

> Were the participant in the delinquent subculture merely employing illicit means to the end of acquiring economic goods, he would show more respect for the goods he has thus acquired. Furthermore, the destructiveness, the versatility, the zest and the wholesale negativism which characterizes the delinquent subculture are beyond the purvue of this theory.

Clearly, in his criticism of the "illicit means" thesis, the reference is to Merton's category of innovation (which involves the use of illegitimate means to conventional goals), and not to anomie theory in general. It is worth noting, that the category of rebellion in Merton's typology *also* does not fit the facts about delinquent subcultures. Rebellion, for Merton, involves the substitution of a new set of goals and means for those being rejected, which resolves the ambivalence. What Cohen describes fits best in the category of *ressentiment* which Merton specifically excludes from his typology altogether. On the other hand, what Cohen describes fits neatly into Parsons' category of rebellion which, it will be recalled, involves ambivalence. Cohen, for reasons which are not evident in his study of gang delinquency, does not acknowledge either of these last two points. The fact that he was a student of

Parsons and, we may assume, familiar with the latter's work on the genesis and directions of deviant motivation, suggests that his emphasis on ambivalence and reaction formation is a product of this familiarity.

Two other aspects of Cohen's thesis deserve comment. Both are ways of looking at the situation within which delinquent subcultures arise that were either de-emphasized or completely overlooked in Merton's original formulation. The first has to do with the process by which deviant solutions to problems of adjustment emerge. The general impression one gets in reading Merton is that a person beset with a problem of adjustment works out a solution to that problem independently of other persons. This model of what happens (referred to by Cohen as a psychogenic model) may suffice, for example, as an explanation for certain kinds of highly individualistic deviant behavior, but it will not suffice as an explanation for the emergence of a delinquent subculture or any other deviant subculture. For Cohen, a sufficient explanation for the emergence of a deviant subculture must recognize the possibility, indeed the probability, of collective problem-solving, involving a high degree of mutuality in the exploration and elaboration of alternatives. In Cohen's own words (1955, p. 61):

> We may think of the process as one of mutual conversion. The important thing to remember is that we do not first convert ourselves and then others. The acceptability of an idea to oneself depends upon its acceptability to others. Converting the other is part of the process of converting oneself.

The second aspect of Cohen's thesis which deserves comment has to do with his recognition that there are class differences in the process of socialization, including the content of what is communicated, and that the degree to which these differences are institutionalized (shared and internalized) is fairly high. His position in this regard is evident in the fact that he does not hesitate to refer to the differences as cultural:

> When we speak of "working-class culture" in the following pages, we shall be speaking of cultural characteristics and emphases which by

no means characterize all working-class families, but which do tend, in a gross statistical sense, to distinguish the cultural milieu of the working-class boy from that of the middle-class boy, and particularly which tend to characterize the least esteemed and economically most insecure levels of the working class (Cohen, 1955, p. 95).

In other words, Cohen recognizes the existence of an established subculture within the lower classes, which has a bearing on the way children socialized in these classes learn to cope with the world. Furthermore, what they learn can affect their behavior independently of structural inequality (a lack of access to legitimate means).

The point at issue here can be approached in another way. If Cohen is correct in his assessment of the situation, it is not simply the lack of access to legitimate means in combination with common success goals which is the source of the problem of adjustment leading to gang delinquency among lower-class males. Also involved is a "socialized inability" on the part of these males to measure up to the standards of success that are being applied to them by people whose "good opinion" is important to them or that have been to some extent internalized, as noted above. The point is important, for if Cohen is correct, access to legitimate means would not *immediately* solve the problem of adjustment faced by lower-class males. In other words, the problem to which Cohen refers includes a lack of access to legitimate means, but it includes more than that. It involves an incapacity which is internal to the actor, a "defect of character," if you will, which puts the lower-class adolescent male at a disadvantage in the race for status even if access to legitimate means were to suddenly increase.

On the other hand, much of what Cohen says implies that over the long haul many of the disabilities among lower-class adolescent males would disappear, if somehow we could eliminate (or even significantly reduce) the inequality of opportunity they face. Moreover, his reasoning, both on the level of general theory and in connection with specific substantive questions, suggests that the lower-class subculture which is responsible for the disabilities, is an adaptation to the relative lack of opportunity faced by lower-class persons generally. For example:

> There is good reason to believe that the modesty of working class aspirations is partly a matter of trimming one's sails to available opportunities and resources (Cohen, 1955, p. 125).

Thus Cohen is saying that the relative lack of access to means which may legitimately be used in attaining culturally favored goals is an important factor in the etiology of the response of the delinquent boy, but it enters the causal sequence in ways which Merton did not consider in any explicit way. It leads to adaptive responses which become established as elements of culture within the lower classes. These elements then affect the ability of lower class adolescent males to live up to the standards of success which are being applied to them and which are sometimes internalized.

In summary, and at the risk of being repetitive, Cohen's contributions to the theory of anomie relate mainly to three aspects of Merton's original formulation. The first has to do with the adequacy of Merton's typology for the analysis of certain forms of deviant behavior, such as gang delinquency. It will be recalled, Cohen argues that the category of innovation, involving the use of illegitimate means to conventional goals, does not fit the facts about the delinquent subculture, in particular, its emphasis on acts of a non-utilitarian or expressive nature. The view expressed herein is that the delinquent subculture, because of the ambivalence which its carriers feel toward the middle-class measuring rod, fits very well into the category of *ressentiment,* which Merton specifically excludes from his typology. For this same reason, the pattern fits rather well into Parsons' category of rebellion. That said, it would be going too far to say, as one author has, that Cohen's criticism of the inadequacy of Merton's typology constitutes a rejection of the theory of anomie. For this and other reasons noted above, Cohen's thesis is best seen as a variant of the theory of anomie as originally formulated by Merton.

The second contribution has to do with the inadequacy of the psychogenic model as an explanation for the emergence of the delinquent subculture or any deviant subculture. Cohen argues convincingly that the psychogenic model in terms of which Merton's theory is constructed does not sufficiently take into account "collective problem-solving," which for Cohen is the basic process by which subcultures are created. The psychogenic model views delinquency as the result of a process of problem solving, but with the implication that each individual solves his problem independently of each other individual. For Cohen this is an inadequate picture of what happens. Indeed, for Cohen, few alterations in "frames of reference" of the type which we associate with social and cultural change would take place if problem solving were of this order. The need for support and the validity which comes from consensus almost require that each person contribute to the solution in a process of mutual conversion, hence his labeling of the process as collective.

The third contribution has to do with several related ideas that Merton neglected or chose not to develop: The problem of adjustment of the lower-class adolescent male is not due simply to a lack of opportunity to compete for certain common success goals, but, in addition, involves a variable that is internal to the actor, namely, the inability to compete effectively even when the opportunity to do so presents itself, which inability is the result of a pattern of socialization within the lower classes. While not central to his theory, this pattern is best seen as an institutionalized response to the relative lack of opportunity faced by lower class persons generally. Thus Cohen's thesis recognizes a variable (the inability to compete effectively) in the development of gang delinquency which, although neglected by Merton, can be traced to the structural variable that figures so prominently in Merton's original formulation of the theory, namely a relative lack of opportunity.

Cloward and Ohlin: Illegitimate Opportunity Structures

It is generally conceded that Cloward and Ohlin are the most significant representatives of that group of anomie theorists who have taken their initial premises from the formulations of Merton (Cf. Clinard, 1964 and Taylor, Walton and Young, 1973). Merton himself (1964, p. 216) assessed their work as constituting the beginning of a new phase in the development of the theory of anomie:

> It is no doubt too soon to say, but I am prepared to make the conjecture that a new phase in the developing theory of anomie was signalled in 1959 by Richard Cloward's paper, which extended the concept of access to the (implicitly legitimate) opportunity structure, a conception further developed in 1960 by Cloward and Lloyd, Ohlin in *Delinquency and Opportunity*.

Actually, Cloward and Ohlin make a number of important contributions to the further development of the theory. All are made in connection with three key questions which their theory attempts to answer. First, what is the source of the problem of adjustment for which delinquent subcultures are attractive solutions? Second, what are the conditions which result in the emergence of delinquent subcultures as solutions? Third, what accounts for the distinctive contents of various delinquent subcultures that have been observed? Our discussion of their contribution will deal with all three questions, but our concern will be mainly with the third, for it is in connection with the question of the basis for the distinctive contents of various delinquent subcultures that the concept of "illegitimate opportunity structures" plays such a prominent part.

Like other anomie theorists, Cloward and Ohlin are concerned with variations in rates of deviance from one category of persons to another. Like Cohen, they start with the assumption that delinquent subcultures are found primarily among lower-class adolescent males. But unlike Cohen they recognize three types of delinquent subcultures, only two of which involve the kinds of expressive or non-utilitarian acts that Cohen argues are a key feature of the culture of the gang. Having recognized three types of delinquent subcultures, they are faced with a theoretical question that Cohen did not face, namely, what accounts for the distinctive contents of these subcultures? In answering this question they, in effect, answer the related question of why they are distributed ecologically in the way that they are.

The facts concerning the three types of delinquent subcultures were collected in the New York City area. With respect to content, the authors observed subcultures that emphasize utilitarian crime (the criminal), others that emphasize the use of drugs (the retreatist), still others that emphasize violence (the conflict). The criminal subculture is broken down into two sub-types, those that emphasize the rackets (the sale of drugs, vice, and gambling) and those that emphasize conventional theft (burglary, larceny, and robbery). With respect to their distribution ecologically (a most important set of facts, as it turns out), the subcultures that emphasize the rackets are found predominantly in Italian neighborhoods, while those that emphasize more conventional theft are found primarily in neighborhoods of mixed nationality. The conflict and retreatist subcultures are found primarily in Black and Puerto Rican neighborhoods.

As already indicated, Cloward and Ohlin take their initial premises from the work of Merton. Indeed, their answer to the first of the questions which they pose (that having to do with the source of the problem of adjustment for which delinquent subcultures are attractive solutions) is substantially the same as that presented by Merton twenty-two years earlier.

> Our hypothesis can be summarized as follows: The disparity between what lower-class youth are led to want and what is actually available to them is the source of a major problem of adjustment. Adolescents who form delinquent subcultures, we suggest, have internalized an emphasis upon conventional goals. Faced with limitations on legitimate avenues of access to these goals, and unable to revise their aspirations downward, they experience intense frustrations; the exploration of nonconformist alternatives may be the result (Cloward and Ohlin, 1960, p. 86).

There are several differences between Cloward and Ohlin's "hypothesis" and the theory of anomie as developed by Merton which this general statement does not reflect. First, the conventional goals to which Cloward and Ohlin refer as having been internalized (and thus converted into aspirations) relate mainly to economic improvement. Lower-class youth who are motivated to join delinquent gangs are not particularly concerned with middle-class status, according to Cloward and Ohlin. Nor do they want to change their life-style. What they want is money and the kind of status within the lower classes that money can provide. Thus the goals with which delinquent types are concerned are conventional goals. And they are goals which are held in common with middle-class youth. But they do not include membership in the middle classes and all that such membership implies in terms of adopting middle-class attitudes and values. Thus also, with respect to conventional goals, Cloward and Ohlin take issue with Cohen.

Second, in an elaboration of their "hypothesis," the authors point out a fact that has been repeatedly substantiated over the years since Merton first presented his version of the theory: That aspirations, on the average, are somewhat lower in the lower classes than in the higher classes.[21] This fact, it should be noted, does not in any sense invalidate the theory of anomie as an explanation for the higher rates of deviance within the lower classes for it is not the level of aspirations that is problematic, but rather the disparity between what lower class persons are led to want and the means available in the pursuit of what they want. Thus, it is the relativity of aspirations which is significant for the theory of anomie, not the level of aspirations in any absolute sense. At the same time it is not insignificant that aspirations vary directly with class. Discontent within the lower classes would be even greater than it is if aspirations at that level were greater than they typically are.

But if the "disparity between what lower class youth are led to want and what is actually available to them" explains the problem of adjustment among lower-class adolescent males, it does not explain the emergence of delinquent subcultures as solutions to this problem, according to Cloward and Ohlin. The authors see four variables as having a bearing on the question of the emergence of delinquent (indeed all deviant) subcultures. First, the persons involved must develop alienative feelings toward, and thus reduce their commitments to, the conventional normative system. The most significant step in the development of alienative feelings toward conventional norms is to come to see those norms as the cause of one's failure rather than, for example, personal inadequacy. Thus "awareness" of the part played by such norms in connection with an individual's success or failure is, therefore, a significant factor in the development of alienative feelings, and beyond that, in the emergence of delinquent subcultures.[22]

Second, the persons involved must be motivated to join with others in attempting to solve their problems rather than to "go it alone." Cloward and Ohlin's argument concerning the source of this motivation is for all practical purposes identical with that presented by Cohen, namely that there are definite advantages to collective problem solving whenever the solution is likely to involve a change in the actor's frame of reference.

> Collective support can provide reassurances, security, and needed validation of a frame of reference toward which the world at large is hostile and disapproving (Cloward and Ohlin, 1960, p. 126).

Third, the persons involved must develop ways of dealing with the guilt which often accompanies participation in activities which contravene conventional norms. It will be recalled that for Parsons and Cohen, guilt in this sense is dealt with by the mechanism of reaction formation. For Cloward and Ohlin (1960, p. 131) the need for such a mechanism is obviated by the process of alienation which, they argue, involves a withdrawal of any feelings of legitimacy toward the conventional norms involved:

> a person who places blame for failure on the unjust organization of the established social order and who finds support from others for his withdrawal of legitimacy from official norms....is psychologically protected against guilt feelings that would otherwise result from violation of those norms.

What they are saying is that the problem of guilt (the unease associated with ambivalence) is solved in advance of the delinquent act, obviating the necessity for defense mechanisms of any kind. Clearly, then, if Cloward and Ohlin are correct, much of the reasoning of Parsons and Cohen (and Merton as well in his discussion of *ressentiment*) on the presence of reaction formation in the genesis of deviant behavior is called into question. Clearly, also, this is an issue that needs further research.

The fourth variable treated by the authors as having a bearing on the development of delinquent subcultures is the presence (or absence) of obstacles to the process of joint problem-solving. In addition to the motivation to solve problems jointly, there must be the opportunity to do so. At the very least there must be effective communication between those who are similarly troubled. This requires as a minimum that they not be physically or socially isolated, factors which need no further elaboration here.

Thus far, we have explained the source of the problem of adjustment for which delinquent subcultures are an attractive solution and the conditions that must be met if the solution is to be a subcultural one. What remains is accounting for the distinctive content of the delinquent subcultures that were observed, the criminal, the conflict, and the retreatist. As noted above, it is in connection with this aspect of their hypothesis that Cloward and Ohlin introduce the concept of an "illegitimate opportunity structure."

Quite simply an "illegitimate opportunity structure" is an established and therefore stable pattern of illegitimate activity which provides opportunities for advancement for those who are exposed to it. Such a pattern is most likely to exist in what Cloward and Ohlin call an "organized slum." By organized, in this context, is meant characterized by a high degree of integration between the non-criminal and criminal value systems, and between the upper-world and under-world residents of the area. It is this high degree of integration, of course, which makes a stable pattern of criminality possible.

Cloward and Ohlin account for the differences in the content of delinquent subcultures by reference to differential access to illegitimate opportunity structures. In those lower-class neighborhoods where there are stable patterns of criminality by which young males can realistically expect to improve their economic status, the delinquent subculture that is most likely to emerge is the "criminal." In such neighborhoods, there are opportunities not only to learn the roles associated with stable patterns of criminality but also to play those roles. There are, in other words, opportunities for engaging in crime as a career. In such neighborhoods, the problem of adjustment creating pressures toward delinquency is likely to be solved by taking advantage of such opportunities.

Conversely, in those neighborhoods where there is no stable pattern of criminality with respect to which a young male can realistically expect to improve his economic status, the criminal pattern is not likely to emerge. In such neighborhoods the risks of getting caught are simply too great. The Harlem area of New York City is a prime example of a "disorganized slum." Even today, (as this is written) there are few, if any, opportunities for blacks to become racketeers. Organized crime is largely controlled by whites, and the police, with whom the racketeers are integrated, see to it that blacks do not become powerful enough to take over the territory. In January of 1960, the discriminatory practices of the police were exposed in a series of articles in the *New York Times*, at which time the Reverend Adam Clayton Powell is quoted as saying:

> There is not operating in Harlem a single banker . . . The entire operation is totally in the hands of people who do not reside in nor are connected with this community. Here we find a community lower in income than any other in the city. And yet we spend $50,000,000 a year to support Italian and Jewish policy bankers (quoted in Cloward and Ohlin, 1960, p. 201).

Earlier in that same month he proclaimed:

> I am against numbers in any form. But, until the day when numbers is wiped out in Harlem—I hate to say this from the pulpit—I am going to fight for the Negro having the same chance as an Italian (quoted in Cloward and Ohlin, 1960, p. 200).

Powell was calling attention to what had been known for some time, that in the New York City area, blacks and Puerto

Ricans lack access to illegitimate as well as legitimate opportunity structures. Under such conditions, according to Cloward and Ohlin, one can expect the frustration to be particularly intense and conflict subcultures to emerge. The thesis is consistent with the facts, as noted earlier: It is in the predominantly black and Puerto Rican neighborhoods that the conflict subculture is most likely to be found.

The retreatist subculture, according to Cloward and Ohlin, develops among the "double failures," those aspiring lower-class youth who fail to achieve their goals either by illegitimate or legitimate means. Retreatism as a pattern involves the substitution of a "kick" (often in the form of drugs) for the status which looms so large in the criminal and conflict gangs. According to Cloward and Ohlin (1960, p. 181) it arises:

> from continued failure to near the goal by legitimate measures and from an inability to use the illegitimate route because of internalized prohibitions or socially structured barriers, this process occurring while the supreme value of the success goal has not yet been renounced.

One of the more important implications of the work of Cloward and Ohlin, especially with respect to their recognition of the significance of illegitimate opportunity structures, is that institutionalized patterns of criminality may be conceived as having positive functional significance for a society in at least two respects. First, they provide opportunities, albeit illegitimate ones, for ambitious lower-class youth to "work their way out of the slums," a fact of considerable significance, as it tends to support the ideology surrounding the American Dream that anybody can "make it" in America if he really tries. Second, were it not for these opportunities they might very well turn to violent activities, which are generally considered more serious, in that they violate personal rather than property rights. An obvious conclusion from all this, of course, is that if we must have anomie, it might be better in terms of consequences, to permit adaptive "criminal" subcultures than to do away with them.

Some Additional Considerations

Earlier it was suggested that perhaps the most serious shortcoming of Merton's work on the theory of anomie has to do with his virtual neglect of two very important questions: What is the functional significance for industrial societies of the practice of emphasizing common success goals? And what is the source of the inequality of opportunity, which is so significant a variable in Merton's explanation of variations in rates of deviance within societies of the American type? The latter question actually has two parts to it: First, what is the source of the inequality in modern societies in the distribution of facilities and rewards? Second, how is this inequality translated into inequality of opportunity? Because of the complexity of the question on the source of inequality of opportunity, we shall deal with it first. Also, by so doing, the question of why modern societies emphasize common success goals will be less difficult to manage.

Achievement Values and Inequality of Rewards

It would seem of the first importance to understand the basis for social inequality if we are to appreciate the complexity of the "problem of anomie" in modern societies and, especially, if we "have a mind to do something about it." Perhaps the clearest statement on the subject may be found in the work of Parsons (1951, pp. 157-61). He argues that in modern (performance-oriented) societies such as our own, there is an "inherent tendency" within "instrumental achievement structures" (organizations producing goods and services) toward differentiation with respect to competence and responsibility, which has implications for social status. Concerning the tendency toward differentiation with respect to competence (defined as the capacity to do things well), Parsons (1951, p. 158) argues as follows:

> achievement values cannot mean anything at all, if there is no discrimination between doing things "well" and doing them "badly".... With any at all elaborate system of the division of labor there will inevitably be a considerable range of differentiation of levels of

competence, especially when a system of different technical roles and not just one role is considered.

Concerning the tendency toward differentiation with respect to responsibility, he argues (1951, p. 159) that:

> beyond rather elementary levels, instrumental role-differentiation requires organization. Organization in turn differentiates roles along the axis of "responsibility" for the affairs of the collectivity. It seems to be one of the best attested empirical generalizations of social science that every continuous organization which involves at all complex cooperative processes, is significantly differentiated along this axis, informally if not formally.

He then goes on to argue that given differences in competence and responsibility we can expect differences in command over facilities, for it would be inefficient, to say the least, to put the best tools in the hands of the least skilled, or the most power (control over the affairs of the organization) into the hands of those with the least responsibility (impossible, actually, because of the relational quality of power). He thus concludes (1951, p. 159) that there is "an inherent tendency to allocate greater facilities to those on the higher levels of competence and responsibility."

There is a tendency toward differentiation, also, with respect to rewards, and for substantially the same reasons. To recognize competence and responsibility as contributing to efficiency is to recognize the value of competence and responsibility. There is thus a tendency for the allocation of rewards to be differentiated along the same lines as the allocation of facilities. In fact, says Parsons (1951, p. 159):

> It is literally impossible to have an instrumental system sanctioned by the valuation of achievement without the internal differentiation of the role and facility structure coming also to be a differentiation of rewards, an internal stratification.

It follows from this that the only way to avoid differentiation in respect to facilities and rewards is to suppress the valuation of competence and responsibility. It follows also that this can be done only at the cost of efficiency. It might be noted in passing that Marxist ideology specifically denies that competence above that displayed by the ordinary worker need be rewarded differentially. But the history of the Soviet experience demonstrates that with respect to both facilities and rewards there has been a high degree of differentiation. The factory manager in the Soviet Union, like his counterpart in the United States, makes substantially more than the ordinary worker. On the other hand, there have been some rather remarkable changes in the direction of equality in the reward structure (if not the facility structure) in the Israeli kibbutz and in the Chinese communes. All such experiments obviously deserve to be studied carefully for evidence that might contradict the theory here being elaborated.

It should be understood that the theory of stratification just described does not even remotely suggest that inequality is inevitable, but only that if a society should want something more than minimal efficiency in the performance of its workers, in whatever capacity they may be working, differentiation on the level of facilities and rewards is important, in fact, necessary. Nor does it suggest that those who possess high status are the best performers, for, as we shall see, status is affected by variables other than efficiency and effectiveness in instrumental achievement structures. Lastly, the rewards and facilities to which the theory makes reference need not be material ones (i.e., material goods or the equivalent in money). Stratification refers to differentiation in the structure of rewards and facilities of any kind. On the other hand, it should be obvious that, in America, material rewards are highly significant ones.

Ascriptive Values and Inequality of Opportunity

It has long been a fundamental feature of the theory of social systems that they are organized around values, and that there is a tendency in such systems toward consistency of action with respect to those values. Also, it is one of the most widely accepted generalizations in social science that the dominant subsystems in American society, the occupational and educational subsystems, are organized around a set of values which emphasize achievement rather than ascription (i.e., what a person *does* rather than who he *is*). Thus one of the crucially important questions for the theorist to answer is why, given the orientation toward achievement within the dominant structures in America and the tendency toward pattern consistency generally in human societies, do we tolerate structural arrangements, such as those associated with kinship systems, which emphasize ascription? We shall attempt to answer the question, but not just because it is of general theoretical significance. The inconsistency to which it refers is part of the reason for inequality of opportunity in modern societies.

The answer lies in understanding, first, that there are two bases for social structure, *any* social structure: The pattern of values by which actors are oriented, and the elements of the situation to which they are oriented. The most important of the situational elements are the so-called functional "exigencies" or "imperatives." In the simplest possible terms, these are the "reality factors" in the situation, the conditions which must be met if the structure is to persist through time.

An obvious implication of this position is that no social structure is derivable from the dominant values alone. Thus, says Parsons (1951, p. 168):

> the extent to which the structure of social systems is not derivable from cultural elements is therefore a measure of the importance of the determinants underlying what we have called the functional "exigencies" or "imperatives" to which they are subject in the realistic conditions of their operation as systems. These resultants of these factors may be considered as patterns of deviation from what would be the model of "perfect integration" in terms of the dominant pattern of value-orientation.

An illustration may serve to illuminate the point Parsons is making. The social structure of American society is a product of certain values or ideals (e.g., men/women should be compensated according to their contributions in terms of goods and services) plus certain situational elements (e.g., the fact that some people are unable to contribute anything in terms of goods and services).

The result is an "operating system" which includes a number of compromises with these values—for example, welfare programs under which men/women get "something for nothing." An important implication of Parsons' position in this regard is that in the absence of these compromises, the system would not survive, which is another way of saying the ideals, in their pure form, are not viable. Parenthetically, according to Parsons, there are no ideals which will meet all of the "needs" of any social system (i.e., all the conditions which must be met if the system is to survive). Parsons (1951, p. 168) refers to the structures which grow out of these compromises as *adaptive structures*. Technically, they are structures which differ in orientation from the dominant structures of the society, but which are nevertheless important (functionally speaking) for the preservation of these structures.

Turning now to the kinship system in modern societies, the reader should not be surprised to learn that it is classified as an adaptive structure. Why? First, because it is different in orientation from the values of the dominant structures of the society and, second, because it is functionally necessary to the preservation of those structures. Actually, it is not correct to say that the kinship system is functionally necessary. What is necessary is that certain functions associated with that system be performed.[23] The function to which we refer is generally thought of as a vital one, which means that the very existence of the society is dependent upon it.

The discussion thus far raises as many questions as it answers. For example, what is the vital function performed by the kinship system (defined as an interactive system based upon biological relatedness), and why must the system which performs this function be oriented around ascriptive rather than achievement values? Concerning the first of these questions, the function to which we refer is the socialization of children. It is generally conceived to be a vital one because no society can long exist without securing a certain level of commitment from new members to its values or, more specifically, to its role structure. Whether this function must be performed within what we have referred to as the kinship system is, of course, open to question. However, as Parsons

(1951, p. 154) has pointed out, there are no known societies in which a major part of the socialization of children does not take place within a unit of the kinship system. Moreover, the socializing agents are strategically important members of such a unit, however it may be defined in a particular society.[24]

Concerning the second of these questions—that having to do with the organization of socialization around ascriptive values—the answer seems to lie in the fact that ascription is an outgrowth of the diffuse love attachments which play such a prominent role in the socialization of children and, indeed, may be necessary for the development of a stable personality.[25] Such attachments, according to Parsons, produce a kind of solidarity in which the facilities and rewards available to one have to be shared with the others. In other words, the solidarity of the kinship unit is likely to push the parents in the direction of treating their loved ones in terms of "who they are rather than what they do," which, in the last analysis, is all that is meant by ascription.

Whatever theoretical considerations one might bring to bear in explaining the universality of ascriptive values within kinship systems, the fact that they are present is of considerable importance to the explanation of inequality of opportunity in modern societies. In summary the argument is as follows: Given the inequality in the facility and reward structure generated by the emphasis on achievement values within productive subsystems, the tendency toward ascription within kinship units means that the children of the successful will have advantages over the children of the unsuccessful. In somewhat more eloquent terms, Parsons (1951, p. 161) puts it as follows:

> In other words, these two basic components of the reward system of the society, occupational approval or esteem and the symbolic accoutrements thereof, and "emotional security," love and response in the kinship unit, must go together in some way. The consequence of this is that the combination of an occupationally differentiated industrial system and a significantly solidary kinship system *must* be a system of stratification in which the children of the more highly placed come to have differential advantages, by virtue of their ascribed kinship status, not shared by those lower down.

Before continuing it seems wise to emphasize several points that, until now, have been mentioned only briefly. First, facilities and rewards can be translated into opportunity by anyone who has access to them, not just by the individual who secured them through meritorious performance or the members of his family, with whom he is likely to share them. Secondly, in some societies of the modern type, notably those with socialist tendencies, the possibility of translating rewards and facilities into opportunities for advancement are far more circumscribed than they are in modern societies of the capitalist type. For example, it is more difficult in socialist than in capitalist societies to translate access to facilities and rewards into educational opportunities for one's children or into investments which by themselves would produce additional rewards. On the other hand, there is some evidence that men who are highly placed in socialist societies do use their power to secure advantages for friends and relatives. This fact is an important theme in a book on socialist bureaucracies (Djilas, 1958). Thus, although a wide range of variation is evident, complete separation of the kinship system from the occupational system, under present conditions, is impossible.

The qualification "under present conditions" in the last sentence is an important one. What we are saying is that we know of no way of socializing children independently of the kinship units which we have been discussing. Utopian thinkers have constructed "ideal" societies in which this is a central feature, Plato's *Republic* and Huxley's *Brave New World* being notable examples, but as yet none has been put into practice. Because of the perceptive way in which Huxley handled the "problem" with which we have been dealing, it deserves further consideration, which we shall give it below.

The Functional Significance of Common Success Goals

The last of the questions with which this part of the chapter is concerned is that having to do with the practice in modern societies of emphasizing common success goals. It will be remembered that the relative lack of opportunity within the lower classes in modern societies would not be problematic if the members of these classes did not share the success goals of the middle and upper classes. It might justifiably be asked, if common success goals are so problematic, if they lead to severe problems of adjustment within the lower classes, why are they emphasized?

The question is not nearly so difficult to answer as it may at first seem. Quite simply, *common success goals provide the motivation for participation in the process by which it is determined who the best performers are.* It will be recalled that the emphasis on achievement values implies recognition of differences in competence and responsibility and, beyond that, in the allocation of rewards. It also implies that the participants in the system are motivated to compete for the rewards which are used to secure competent and responsible performance. This motivation can be guaranteed only if the persons involved here to some extent become committed to the acquisition of the commodities that have been defined as rewards. In the American case, these commodities are, in effect, the culturally favored goals. The line of reasoning involved here should not be taken to mean that all persons in America are committed to these goals. In fact, there is considerable evidence to suggest that they are not.[26] However— and this is the point at issue—those who are not committed are not motivated to compete, at least in terms of the goals in question. A good example of the type of person we have in mind here is the societal dropout, of which the hippie might be seen as an obvious example.

Where We Stand

Putting it all together, where do we stand? What is the present state of our thinking on the theory of anomie? The following series of propositions should serve to answer the question. Emphasis is given to those ideas most relevant to the discussion of the implications for change which follows.

1. Anomie is best conceived as widespread disrespect for one or more aspects of a society's normative system. However,

because it is a function of certain structural features of modern societies, the disrespect can be seen as a sociological phenomenon.
2. Anomie is the result of several combinations of what appear to be unavoidable structural features of modern societies. The most important of these are (1) the emphasis on achievement values (performance) within the productive subsystem, (2) the de-emphasis within this same system on norms prescribing legitimate means to socially prescribed goals and, (3) the emphasis within the kinship subsystem on ascriptive values
3. Actually, these structural features combine to produce anomie in two different but related ways. The emphasis on achievement values within the productive subsystem is a source of anomie in that it stresses goal-attainment rather more than conformity to the norms prescribing legitimate means to those goals. This source of anomie explains the higher rates of deviance in societies of the American type as compared with societies of the "ritualistic" type. Merton explicitly recognizes this source of anomie in his original treatment of the subject.
4. The emphasis on achievement values within the productive subsystem *in combination with* the emphasis on ascriptive values within the kinship subsystem produces anomie by stressing goal-attainment even among those who possess a relative lack of access to the means which may legitimately be used in pursuing the approved goals. This "relative lack of access" is a function in large part of the presence within the kinship system of ascriptive values, which means that the rewards of success are likely to be shared with loved ones. This source of anomie explains the higher rates of deviance in the lower as compared with the higher classes within societies of the American type.
5. The emphasis on achievement values within the productive subsystems of modern societies is by no means accidental. The stress in these subsystems on efficiency *requires* an emphasis on achievement values. The de-emphasis on norms prescribing legitimate means is also a function of the orga-

nization of modern societies because of the value placed on progressive social change, the latter being possible only when there is a great deal of flexibility in the normative system.
6. To say that a society emphasizes achievement values is to say simply that it stresses what a person does (his performance) rather than who he is (his qualities).
7. The stress on performance requires that good performers be given something more than bad performers. What they are given can be a material reward or a non-material reward or some combination of the two, but whatever they are given, the result will be inequality in status as between those who perform well and those who do not. It should be obvious that one cannot infer from this fact that all those who possess high status, even in an achievement oriented society, are the best performers, for as stated above, ascriptive values within the kinship system may mean that a person's status may be a function of one's relations within that system, rather more than one's performance. The emphasis on performance also means that access to facilities will also be distributed unequally and this too can produce inequality in status among relatives.
8. Though often ignored, a relative lack of opportunity by itself is not a source of anomie. It is only when the disadvantages of class are combined with an emphasis on common success goals that anomie is likely to develop within the lower classes.
9. The function of common success goals is a point on which there is considerable agreement among anomie theorists. Common success goals provide the motivation for the competition without which it would be difficult (if not impossible) to ascertain who are the best performers.
10. The facilities and rewards associated with high status can usually be translated into some kind of opportunity for acquiring even greater rewards (i.e., for advancement within the status hierarchy). This is so not only for the person who receives the rewards, but for others as well, if he chooses to share them. In the American case, the ascriptive values within the kinship subsystem virtually dictate that the person who receives the

rewards share them with his family. This explains why the children of the successful have advantages over the children of the unsuccessful.

11. The rewards associated with high status can be more easily translated into opportunity for others in capitalistic societies than in socialistic ones. This kind of translation is a function of the freedom which exists in America to invest in education, in business enterprises, etc. Socialist societies greatly restrict this freedom, so that inequality of opportunity in socialist societies is less than in capitalistic societies. However, it is not unknown in such societies.

12. Inequality of opportunity (in combination with an emphasis on common success goals) produces anomie in part because the person who fails to attain the approved goals can (depending upon his level of awareness) "make a case" for that failure as being due to "structural features of the system" rather than to his own incapacity. Thus his "level of awareness" must be regarded as a significant variable explaining differential rates of anomie by social class.

13. Regardless of the source of anomie, its existence is likely to lead to deviance as a solution to the problems which it presents. It does not follow, however, that only anomie can lead to deviance. There are undoubtedly other sources as well.

14. The dynamics of the way in which the state of anomie leads to deviance is an area in which further theoretical development is needed, but the work of Parsons, Cohen, and Cloward and Ohlin constitutes an important step in the direction of solving the problems that still exist.

15. Anomie theory implies that ambivalence is likely to be present in the motivational patterns of persons who have developed disrespect for one or more aspects of a society's normative pattern. This is because the disrespect is a function of participation in the society whose norms the actor comes to disrespect and, further, that participation implies some degree of internalization of the problematic normative pattern.

16. Agreement is not nearly so great on the question of how the negative component of the ambivalent motivational structure is managed. For Parsons and Cohen it is managed by a process of repression resulting in reaction formation; for Cloward and Ohlin it is managed by a process of learning involving the substitution of a new set of normative standards.
17. Until recently, discussions of the process by which solutions were arrived at made little reference to interaction between "kindred souls"—persons who are similarly troubled. It was as if each person arrived at his solution independently of each other. Now, the weight of opinion is on the side of those who argue that, while some solutions may be arrived at in this way, those which become institutionalized as subcultures are created collectively.
18. In recognizing that some solutions become institutionalized as subcultures, anomie theorists have come to see the complexity of the process by which deviance is generated. The process is now conceived as involving, in addition to the basic problematic variables, or more institutionalized subcultures which combine to produce the deviant solution. For example, a lower class culture, adaptive though it may be, can nevertheless be seen as contributing (in the way Cohen suggests) to the problems faced by lower-class adolescent males.
19. These solutions, when institutionalized, are what Parsons calls "adaptive structures." They are structures which stress values that depart from a dominant pattern, but which nevertheless have positive functional significance in relation to the dominant pattern. Among lower class adolescents, they co-opt, cool out, buy off the dissidents, often by providing outlets which are less disruptive than if the actors involved were to deviate from the dominant pattern.
20. Such structures, of course, become important variables in explaining why some persons do not succeed, even when opportunities develop. For example, if such structures reduce aspirations or promise rewards in the hereafter for suffering on earth, those who are involved in them are less likely to

take advantage of opportunities for advancement which may develop.

Implications for Change

It is often said that sociologists are willing to analyze the situation surrounding social problems, but unwilling to propose solutions. True or not, the statement describes a position which should be understandable to anyone who is familiar with the limitations of science in connection with matters of social policy and with the role of scientist as neutral observer. Logically, as most philosophers will readily admit, science is a limited mode of cognition, which means that although science can tell us what is and what might be on the basis of what is, it cannot tell us what is right (or wrong) in any ultimate sense of the term. Because of this limitation, sociologists *as scientists* have been reluctant to get involved in matters of social policy, which in one way or another involve judgments of ultimate value. On the other hand, sociologists, *as citizens*, have been willing to discuss the implications of their theories for change whenever it appears that specific changes may eliminate a condition that is considered problematic for the society and whenever it is understood that in discussing such changes no judgments of ultimate value are intended, i.e., when it is understood that no one change is considered any better in an ultimate sense than any other. It is this latter set of considerations which underlies our motivation here.

Actually, the inclusion of a section on "implications for change" of the theory of anomie as an explanation for deviance in America is based upon several considerations. First, as already suggested, it would seem to be the responsible thing to do, given the seriousness of the problem of crime and social unrest in America today. But there is another reason as well, which might serve to justify the exercise. An in-depth discussion of change as a solution is likely to reveal information on the costs involved in eliminating the conditions presumably responsible for the problem. Such information, it is felt, can be of value in at least two respects: It can help us make more rational judgments on solutions, and it can make us more aware of what one must "give up" in order to "solve" the problem—and give up something we must, whenever a social arrangement is altered. At the very least, we must give up an established way of doing things and the gratification which accompanies participation in such ways. More important, almost any change will have implications for the satisfaction of economic and political interests, by which is meant that the change will involve a shift in the distribution of money and power. In other words, a discussion of the "implications for change" of the theory of anomie can be expected to reveal the "political-economy" of the problem. From our point of view, revelations of this sort are quite desirable, if for no other reason than that they suggest the sources, on the one hand, of resistance to a given solution and, on the other, of support for that solution.

Whatever the value of a section on "implications for change," the discussion will take the form of describing certain changes which can be expected to reduce the degree of anomie and thus the consequences in terms of deviance. There will be no concern with what is political feasible, i.e., acceptable to a majority of the American people. Indeed, it is assumed that most of the changes to be discussed would not be politically feasible, at least at this stage in our history. More important, there will be no concern for measures of the type classified by sociologists as mechanisms of social control. Concern will be with changes in organization which can be expected to result in the production of less anomie, and not with measures which can be expected to control the expressions of that condition after it has been produced. For example, there will be no concern either with deterrence (through threats of punishment) or with therapy (through changes in the structure of personality), both of which are strategies of control. This is not to imply that strategies of control do not in some sense "work," but only that our concern is with changes in the structure of the social system which gives rise to the problem.

The first of the changes to be considered relates directly to Merton's contention that a major source of anomie in American society is the relatively greater emphasis on goal-attainment than on conformity to the norms prescribing legitimate means. It follows from this assumption that anomie and the tendencies toward deviance associated with it, in so far as they are a result of this combination of variables, can be reduced by changes in social structure which would produce a more "integrated" society, i.e., one in which there is a "rough balance between emphases upon cultural goals and institutionalized practices" (Merton, 1957, p. 134). In such a society, it will be recalled, the pressure to attain the cultural goals is less intense than in societies of the American type, and there is a greater sense of satisfaction simply from participating in competitive activity.

It follows also that anomie and the tendencies toward deviance associated with it could be virtually eliminated by changes which would produce a ritualistic society. In such a society, it will be recalled, there is a relative lack of concern for goal-attainment, so that satisfactions are almost exclusively a function of participation in competitive activity. Actually, it is quite likely that in a ritualistic society there would be no competitive activity as we know it in America, because with a relative lack of concern for goal-attainment, "winning" would have little meaning.

In contemplating ritualism as a solution, it should be remembered that, according to Merton, societies at the ritualistic end of the continuum are no less "malintegrated" than societies of the American type. The difference lies in the problem they face. In ritualistic societies the problem is not one of anomie, but of rigidity and the consequences thereof in terms of the inability to adjust to changing life-conditions. The problem faced by ritualistic societies was very well put some years ago in *Time* (1964), in an analysis of the situation faced by India when China exploded its first atomic device.

> Of all the Asian nations affected by Peking's nuclear explosion, India has the most to fear. Since Red China's humiliating walk through the Himalayas in 1962, the Indians have been obsessed by fear of renewed Communist aggression. Thus, though India was only recently the antinuclear Cassandra of the nonaligned world, the nation last week was earnestly debating whether to build A-bombs of its own.
> Chief problem of India's nuclear advocates, of course, is their na-

tion's deep emotional attachment to the principles of nonviolence, as practiced by Ghandi and internationally canonized by the late Jawaharlal Nehru. In a speech to students last week, Lal Bahadur Shastri, Nehru's successor, loyally insisted: "We cannot change our conviction because of China's action."

The fact that India subsequently proceeded to build A-bombs of its own and proved to be flexible enough to adjust to what was conceived to be a serious threat to the nation's survival does not invalidate the point at issue, namely, that ritualism, like anomie, may have serious consequences for a society.

Returning to the less radical move of structuring a more "integrated" society, the consequences, though less threatening to national survival, are no less important for present purposes. Because of the close functional relationship between goal-attainment and the average level of performance, one would expect a de-emphasis upon the former to have a depressing effect upon the latter. Indeed, if it may be argued that anomie is the cost of the relatively greater emphasis on goal-attainment than on conformity to legitimate means, then a reduction in the average level of performance is the cost of any change in social structure which would produce a more "integrated" society. Put somewhat differently, with less emphasis on goal-attainment and more emphasis on conformity to institutional means, the concern would be less with "winning," more with "how one plays the game."

The impact of such a change in emphasis is very likely to be greatest within the productive subsystem of a society of the American type (also within the educational subsystem which is closely tied to it), although a change of this type is likely to affect all those subsystems in which there is a strong performance orientation. Moreover—and this is no less important a consideration—it is likely to affect persons at all class levels, since it involves a change in orientation of the society generally. Translated into economic terms, the change being discussed would, other things remaining equal, reduce the rate at which productivity has been increasing and, therefore, the level of material well-being. The level of productivity must certainly be highly dependent upon the emphasis on performance as measured by the norms of efficiency and effectiveness.

Less obvious perhaps, but equally important, is the depressing effect which such a change would have on the rate of innovation in American society. Whatever one's concept of moral and economic progress, the ability to innovate is essential to its attainment. The relationship between the variables involved can be seen in the following statement by Durkheim (1964a) who was particularly concerned with the conditions that facilitate change in the moral norms:

> [I]n order that these transformations *[in moral norms]* may be possible, the collective sentiments as the basis of morality must not be hostile to change, and consequently must have moderate energy. If they were too strong, they would no longer be plastic. Every pattern is an obstacle to new patterns, to the extent that the first is inflexible (p. 70).

Thus,

> The authority which the moral conscience enjoys must not be excessive; otherwise no one would dare criticize it, and it would be too easily congeal into an immutable form. To make progress, individuality must be able to express itself. In order that the originality of the idealist whose dreams transcend his century may find expression, it is necessary that the originality of the criminal, who is below the level of his time, shall also be possible (p. 71).

In other words, the conditions which allow for desirable innovation also allow for undesirable innovation. Or, what is the same thing, the conditions which prevent undesirable innovation also prevent desirable innovation.

Another change implied by our summary formulation of the theory relates directly to Merton's contention that a second source of anomie lies in the disparity between the commitment of lower-class persons to common success goals and their relative lack of access to the means which may legitimately be used in pursuing those goals. It follows from Merton's contention that anomie from this source (and the deviance associated with it) can be reduced either by reducing the commitment of lower-class persons to common success goals, or by increasing their access to the means which may legitimately be used in pursuing those goals or by some combination of the two.

Again, if our theory is correct, the first of these moves—reducing the commitment of lower-class persons to common success goals—can be expected to reduce the motivation of lower-class persons to succeed and, along with it, the quality of their performance. However, it might be expected to have a similar effect in the higher classes as well, if it results in a decline in the number of lower-class persons who are motivated to compete for the cultural goals. As the number of persons competing for these goals declines, the need to perform among those who remain would be reduced. In other words, as their status becomes more secure, higher-class persons can be expected to be less concerned with performance.

It should be obvious that any reduction in commitment among lower-class persons to common success goals will decrease the rate of upward social mobility of lower-class persons. In turn, this means a reduction in the rate at which talent (performance capabilities) within the lower classes will be developed and utilized. This probable consequence, it might be noted, has been seized upon by some theories as the one which the emphasis on competition and on common success goals is designed to avoid.[27] It might be wise at this time to examine more closely what such theorists have been saying.

Their argument may be stated as follows: The pattern of competition and the emphasis on common success goals associated with it have arisen in industrial societies to meet a need in such societies for a high level of performance, especially in connection with the more technical work roles. Competition, although obviously not without drawbacks, appears on balance to be the most efficient way of allocating persons to such roles. How? By insuring a high degree of correspondence between the demands of such work roles and the performance capabilities of the persons being "allocated." Put another way, were an industrial society to depend upon a system of ascription, based, let us say, on kinship relationships, which are not necessarily related to performance, the allocation of persons to work roles would be much less efficient. There is no assurance, for example, that the son of a lab technician, by virtue of that fact, will be capable or willing to "fill his parent's shoes."

An interesting implication of this kind of reasoning is that if somehow one could predict at birth who would and who would not later on possess the talent and motivation necessary to perform effectively in various technical work roles, assignment to those roles could be made at birth, and the system of competition, with its emphasis on common success goals, could be eliminated. To get this kind of predictability, of course, would require far more knowledge of and/or control over the processes of reproduction and socialization than now exists.

The kind of knowledge and/or control required was described some years ago in Huxley's *Brave New World* (1932), apparently without any intention of suggesting a way one might solve the problem of anomie. Briefly, what he depicted was a society in which the reproduction and socialization of children were carried out "scientifically" on assembly-lines and in nurseries. The processes they used produced precisely the right number of qualified persons for each level of work role in the society. Everyone was able and willing (motivated) to do the job he was assigned to do, and no one had more ability or motivation than was required for his job.

Clearly this is a kind of "ideal" solution to the problem of anomie in that it permits the elimination of the frustrations associated with the present system of competition without reducing the high average level of performance which it produces. Whether we shall ever acquire the degree of control over reproduction and socialization described by Huxley remains to be seen. This author thinks it is very unlikely, in spite of a great deal of speculation to the contrary. On the other hand, should the technology someday be developed which would permit a high level of control over these processes, there is little doubt in his mind that it will be utilized for the solution of problems such as the one with which we are here concerned.

Perhaps the most frequently proposed solution to the "problem" of anomie within the lower classes is that of increasing the access of persons at this level to the means which may legitimately be used in attaining the cultural goals. Logically, this can be done in at least two ways: By leveling all occupations, according them equal rewards, and by retaining inequality in the reward structure while making it difficult to translate this inequality in rewards into inequality of opportunity for oneself and others.

Concerning the first of these approaches, leveling all occupations, such a change could be expected to reduce inequality of opportunity, since there would be no inequality in rewards to translate into inequality of opportunity. However, because of the functional significance of inequality in the reward structure for the motivation of performance, it could be expected also to reduce the average level of performance within those subsystems emphasizing performance, and at all class levels. In addition, such a change would very likely make it more difficult to fill positions of responsibility at the top of the hierarchy of occupations, since to make the sacrifices involved in preparing for them would no longer "pay." As indicated earlier, equality in the reward structure is part of the program for reform of the Marxists, but seems to be inconsistent with their belief in industrialization and the related emphasis on performance.

Concerning the second of these approaches, retaining the emphasis on inequality within the reward structure while making it difficult to translate this inequality in rewards into inequality of opportunity, implementation would require that the successful performers be restricted in the use of the rewards for that performance to the purchase of consumer goods (and services). It would be necessary to control the use of rewards for "investments" which would yield some kind of advantage (in relation to various success goals) without additional effort by the investor. This could be accomplished in America only by the elimination of the private ownership of capital goods and by equalizing educational opportunities. It is this approach which is most consistent with the goals, if not the actual practices, of many socialist countries, notably the Soviet Union.

There is at least one additional point worth making with respect to this approach to the equalization of opportunity: It would not eliminate the frustrations associated with competition, especially for certain categories of individuals. As one author (Johnson, 1960, p. 574) put it some years ago:

> [A]ttempts to equalize opportunity, while desirable for their own sake within the American value system, would not necessarily reduce the competitive strain for those whose native endowments or unusual personal experiences unfit them for successful competition. Further, the social structure itself has a limited number of positions at the top, and some people would have to "fail" even all were equally able.

There is an implication of this line of reasoning which is worth exploring. It seems clear that the "advantage" of equality of opportunity for the society is that it makes difficult any attempt by those who fail to blame the system for that failure. The problem of adjustment for those who fail would very likely be, therefore, resolved in the direction of blaming oneself rather than the system. And while it may be assumed that a tendency toward blaming oneself is likely to result in higher rates of mental illness and of suicide, neither of these is as threatening to the society as the consequences of blaming the system.

It should not be forgotten that, in the American case, by eliminating the disparity between goals and means, only one of the two sources of anomie is removed; there remains the emphasis on goal-attainment which puts a strain on the institutional controls over the use of illegitimate means. Thus any serious effort to reduce the level of anomie in American society would of necessity involve a move toward a more "integrated" society in Merton's terms.

Before concluding the section on "implications for change," it is important to point out that to argue, as we have, that it is possible through changes in social structure to reduce the rates of deviant behavior, this should not be taken to mean that we believe that through such changes (or any others, for that matter) deviance can be eliminated from human society. Society is a moral order, which means its boundaries are defined by moral norms, and so long as this is the case, what is defined as deviance at any given time can be eliminated only by the most successful kind of socialization. The norms would have to be implanted uniformly in all individuals and with sufficient intensity to deter the expression of all desires to the contrary. In his treatment of this very subject, Durkheim (1946a, p. 69) argued that:

> [A] uniformity so universal and absolute is utterly impossible; for the immediate physical mileu in which each one of us is placed, the hereditary antecedents, and the social influences vary from one individual to the next, and consequently diversify consciousnesses. It is impossible for all to be alike, if only because each one has his own organism and these organisms occupy different areas in space.

What is more important, even if it were possible through a process of socialization to deter the expression of all motivation to engage in what is now defined as deviant behavior, the very process by which this is accomplished would create new categories of deviance. Durkheim's discussion of the inevitability of crime provides us with the logic for this conclusion (1964a, p. 68):

> One easily overlooks the consideration that these strong states of the common consciousness cannot be reinforced without reinforcing at the same time the more feeble states, whose violation previously gave birth to mere infraction of convention—since the weaker ones are only the prolongation, the attenuated form, of the stronger. Thus robbery and simple bad taste injure the same single altruistic sentiment, the respect for that which is another's. However, this same sentiment is less grievously offended by bad taste than by robbery; and since, in addition, the average consciousness has not sufficient intensity to react keenly to the bad taste, it is treated with greater tolerance. That is why the person guilty of bad taste is merely blamed, whereas the thief is punished. But if this sentiment grows stronger, to the point of silencing in all consciousnesses the inclination which disposes man to steal, he will become more sensitive to the offenses which, until then, touched him but lightly. He will react against them, then, with more energy; they will be the object of greater opprobrium, which will transform certain of them from the simple moral faults that they were and give them the quality of crimes.

What he is saying, in other words, is that by strengthening the sentiments supporting the moral norms, the result may well be a reduction in the number of acts which offend these norms, from the most serious to the least serious. But as a result of the very same process (i.e., by strengthening the sentiments supporting the moral norms) there is likely to be another result as well: The definition of what is criminal will change in the direction of including acts that were before "simple moral faults." By carrying this logic one step further, it may be concluded that by strengthening the sentiments supporting the moral norms, acts that were once tolerated as acceptable departures from the moral norms will become unacceptable.

What this means, if it is not already clear, is that deviance, like crime, is inevitable, a consequence of the institutionalization of a set of moral norms. Thus, it is the product of the very process by which order in human societies is secured. The "problem" stems from the fact that the moral norms not only function to control behavior within the categories covered by those norms, they define the categories. That is why attempts to reduce the number of violations under a given set of norms by strengthening the supporting sentiments may be quite successful, but at the same time may have the consequence of expanding the definition of what constitutes an intolerable violation. That is why the process by which humans attempt to secure order appears doomed to failure; the gains made in one area of activity are lost in another.

Returning to our discussion of the implications of the theory of anomie for social change (as a solution to the problem of deviance), it may be concluded from all this that even in a society characterized by a low level of anomie, there will nevertheless be some deviance. But by the same token it may be concluded that a society characterized by a high level of anomie will have a great deal more deviance. It is this added increment of deviance with which we are concerned in the present section, and to which the changes under discussion refer. Our concern is not with deviance in general, but with that deviance generated by the phenomenon of anomie.

If there is any one conclusion of this discussion that is worth stating, it is that the problems which societies face are sometimes a function of mechanisms which have been created by these societies to meet the conditions of their own existence. Anomie may be seen as one such problem. At the risk of being repetitious, anomie may be seen as a product of the attempt by industrial societies (for example, through a system of competition) to meet a need for a high level of performance in connection with the more technical work roles. Industrial societies thus face a dilemma: They can eliminate anomie only by recreating the problem for which the pattern of competition is a solution. If it is indeed a dilemma, then there is no completely satisfactory solution; there is only the possibility of a "trade off" of one combination of good and evil for another. In this connection, science can be of some value in specifying the alternatives of action that are open to such societies and in estimating the costs associated with these alternatives, but it cannot resolve the questions of ultimate value involved in the trade-off decision. It is possible, of course, that science may produce the technology noted earlier in the discussion of *Brave New World*, but even if it does, decisions of ultimate value must be made regarding the use of such technology.

There is one other approach to the dilemma which should be noted. We can continue, as we have, to do nothing about the source of anomie and the motivation to deviance and concentrate on its control through the strategies of deterrence and therapy. Although costly, social control does have one distinct "advantage," it requires no fundamental changes in the system which lies at the root of the problem.

Bibliography

Becker, Howard S.
    1963   *Outsiders: Studies in the Sociology of Deviance,* New York: Free Press.

Clinard, Marshall B.
    1964   *Anomie and Deviant Behavior,* New York: Free Press.

Cloward, Richard and Ohlin, Lloyd
    1960   *Delinquency and Opportunity: A Theory of Delinquent Gangs,* New York: Free Press.

Cohen, Albert K.
    1955   *Delinquent Boys: The Culture of the Gang,* New York: Free Press.
    1965   "The Sociology of the Deviant Act: Anomie Theory and Beyond," *American Sociological Review,* Vol. 30.
    1966   *Deviance and Social Control,* New Jersey: Prentice Hall.

Davis, Kinsley
    1940   "Extreme Isolation of a Child" in *American Journal of Sociology,* Vol. 45.

Djilas, Milovan
    1957   *The New Class: An Analysis of the Communist System,* New York: Praegar.

Durkheim, Emile
    1951   *Suicide: A Study in Sociology,* New York: Free Press.
    1964a   *Rules of Sociological Method,* New York: Free Press.
    1964b   *The Division of Labor in Society,* New York: Free Press.

Gouldner, Alvin W.
    1970   *The Coming Crisis of Western Sociology,* London: Heinemann Educational.

Horton, John
    1964   "The Dehumanization of Anomie and Alienation: A Problem in the Ideology of Sociology," *British Journal of Sociology,* Vol. 15.

Huxley, Aldous
    1932   *Brave New World,* New York: Doubleday, Doran and Company, Inc.

Johnson, Harry M.
    1960   *Sociology: A Systematic Introduction,* New York: Harcourt Brace and World, Inc.

Kerbo, Harold
    1973   *System Blaming as a Function of Density, Relative Deprivation, Ideology and Ethnicity,* University of Oklahoma, Unpublished Master's Thesis

Merton, R. K.
    1957   *Social Theory and Social Structure (revised edition),* New York: Free Press.
    1964   "Anomie, Anomia and Social Interaction: Contexts of Deviant Behavior," in Marshall B. Clinard, *Anomie and Deviant Behavior,* New York: Free Press.
    1971   "Social problems and Sociological Theory" in Merton, R. K. and Nisbet, Robert, *Contemporary Social Problems,* New York: Harcourt Brace Jovanovich, Inc.

Murdock, George P.
    1949   *Social Structure,* New York: Macmillan.

Parsons, Talcott
    1949   *The Structure of Social Action,* New York: Free Press.
    1951   *The Social System,* New York: Free Press.

Spitz, Rene
    1945   "Hospitalism" in *Psychoanalytic Study of the Child,* Vols. I and II, New York
    1946   International Universities Press. Taylor, Walton, and Young

Taylor, Walton, and Young
    1973   *The New Criminology,* London: Routledge and Kegan Paul Lts.

Time Magazine
    1964   *Vol. 84,* November 6.

Whitman, Walt
    1870   *Democratic Vistas,* New York: J. S. Redfield.

End Notes

1. For summary statements of the statistics bearing on the magnitude of these problems, see the President's Commission on Law Enforcement and Administration of Justice, *Task Force Report: Crime and Its Impact—An Assessment* (Washington, U.S. Government Printing Office, 1967), *Report of the National Advisory Commission on Civil Disorders* (Washington, U.S. Government Printing Office, 1968) and *To Establish Justice, To Insure Domestic Tranquility* (Washington, U.S. Government Printing Office, 1970).

2. For an excellent discussion of the history of violence in America, see *To Establish Justice, to Insure Domestic Tranquility* (Washington, U.S. Government Printing Office, 1970) Chapter I, "Violence in American History."

3. For an extended list of studies which utilize the concept of anomie, see the "Inventory of Empirical Studies," by Stephen Cole and Harriet Zuckerman in *Anomie and Deviant Behavior*, edited by Marshall B. Clinard (New York, The Free Press of Glencoe, 1964), pp. 246-89.

4. The original version of the article was published in *The American Sociological Review*, Volume 3, pp. 672-82. It has been reprinted in Merton's *Social Theory and Social Structure* (Revised Edition, New York, The Free Press of Glencoe, 1957), pp. 131-60.

5. Two works by Durkheim are significant in this regard: *The Division of Labor in Society*, translated by George Simpson (New York, The Free Press of Glencoe, 1964) and *Suicide*, translated by John Spaulding and George Simpson (New York, The Free Press of Glencoe, 1951).

6. For discussion of the "evil-causes evil" fallacy and the impact of this kind of thinking on the development of sociological theory, see Albert K. Cohen, "Multiple Factor Approaches" in Wolfgang, Savitz, and Johnson, *The Sociology of Crime and Delinquency* (New York, John Wiley and Sons, 1970) pp. 123-26.

7. Cf. Gouldner, 1970, pp. 65-73.

8. It might be noted that the "sociological" as compared with the "clinical" approach is not just another way of analyzing the same variables. Often the sociological approach will ignore variables considered important in the clinical approach, if it appears that they bear only on the explanation of the incidence of the phenomenon under the examination. The point can perhaps best be made by reference to an illustration. Differences in GRE scores might well explain why one student gets into graduate school while another does not, but it is extremely unlikely that changes in GRE scores would explain the increases or decreases in graduate enrollment which can be observed from time to time.

9. It has been argued that what Durkheim in effect does in recognizing the dynamics of the Protestant case is abandon his claim in *The Division of Labor* that organic solidarity involves a significant reduction of the collective conscience, and move toward a position which permits us to see organic solidarity as involving not the absence of a collective conscience but the substitution of a new collective conscience for the old one. In the industrial west, it involves the doctrine of individualism, with its obligation to be free of all sorts of religious, domestic, or political restraints, but at the same time to be moral in ways that are consistent with the needs of an industrial society. For an elaboration of this view, see T. Parsons, *The Structure of Social Action* (New York, The Free Press of Glencoe, 1949) pp. 324-38.

10. It is important to keep in mind what was mentioned earlier: that anomie is conceived quite differently in *Suicide* than it is in *The Division of Labor*.

11. For the sociologist interested in such questions, it is suggested that the answer may lie in the fact that Merton's thesis in this regard implies that anomie is an inevitable consequence of the most basic features of the American Way, an idea which only the most detached observers of the American scene care to contemplate. It may lie also in the fact that many sociologists apparently believe that the structural features which give rise to deviant behavior within societies of the American type can be eliminated without making basic changes in the American way. Indeed, they may feel that these features would not exist if the members of American society would only live up to its

ideals, notably that of equality of opportunity. It is an implication of the thesis of the present chapter that this ideal can be realized, if at all, only by making radical changes in the American Way. Thus Merton's thesis on the consequences of inequality of opportunity in generating deviance is just as devastating a critique of the American Way, when all of its implications are made clear, as is his thesis on the consequences of the emphasis on success in societies of the American type without an equivalent emphasis on institutional means.

12. Other interpretations of Durkheim's concept of anomie are no doubt possible. For example, one could conceive of the expediency on the level of means as violating the norms which presumably existed prior to advances in the division of labor, which conception would justify arguing that even in the context of *The Division of Labor,* anomie involves deviance. But this interpretation rests on the assumption that the collective conscience underlying the solidarity of the preindustrial state of society has not been destroyed. If we take Durkheim as his word, advances in the division of labor inevitably lead to the destruction of the collective conscience.

13. See, for example, Cohen, 1955.

14. In this connection, one is reminded of the attitude toward success which surrounds big-time college football—namely, that there is only one "winner," the number one team in the nation, and that all the rest are "losers."

15. See, for example, Richard Austin Smith, "The Incredible Electrical Conspiracy," *Fortune* (April, 1961), pp. 132-80 and (May, 1961), pp. 161-244; Daniel Bell, "Crime as an American Way of Life," *The Antioch Review* (June, 1953), pp. 131-54; Edward H. Sutherland, *White Collar Crime*, New York, Holt, Rinehard and Winston, 1949; Robert A. Lane, "Why Business Men Violate the Law," *Journal of Criminal Law, Criminology and Police Science*, 44 (August, 1953), pp. 151-65.

16. The concept of reaction formation is discussed in detail below, in connection with the contributions to the theory of anomie of Talcott Parsons.

17. If this statement is to be taken literally, it would be more accurate to view rebellion not as deviance from the conventional system of values against which the actor is said to be rebelling, but conformity to an alternative system, as stated earlier. Indeed, Merton himself seems to be taking a position similar to this in a recent statement on the subject in which he classifies rebellion as non-conformity, while continuing to see the other modes of adaptation as aberrant forms of behavior. At the same time, the existence of the alternative system of values may be viewed as the result of reaction against the conventional normative system which is seen as problematic. (Merton, 1971, pp. 829-32)

18. See the discussion of Cohen's views below.

19. See, for example, Clinard, 1964, pp. 30-33 and Taylor, Walton and Young, 1973, pp. 135-38.

20. They appeared later in several other publications as well. (See, for example, Cohen, 1965 and 1966.)

21. Several of the more important studies on the subject are summarized in Cloward and Ohlin (1960, pp. 87-90).

22. System-blaming versus self-blaming has only recently received the attention it deserves as a variable affecting the development of alienative feelings, even though a

case for research on the subject was made by Merton (1957, p. 240) some years ago. For a good summary of the literature bearing on the subject and for the results of an important piece of research on factors affecting the tendency toward system-blaming, see Kerbo (1972).

23. There may be other equally necessary functions performed by the kinship system, but for the purposes of simplifying the discussion, only one such function will be treated. For an introduction to the more important concepts and issues surrounding functional analysis, see Johnson (1960, Chapter 3).

24. For data substantiating these generalizations, see Murdock (1949).

25. For evidence concerning the functional significance of diffuse love attachments, see Spitz (1945-46, Vols. I & II) and Davis (1940, pp. 554-64).

26. For a good discussion of the literature on the subject, see Cloward and Ohlin (1960, pp. 86-97).

Representations of Merton's Theory of Anomie*

R.E. Hilbert & Charles W. Wright

Merton's famous statement, "Social Structure and Anomie" points to two sources of strain in the genesis of deviance in societies of the American type: (1) emphasis on goals over means, and (2) lack of access to legitimate means. We have observed through a central analysis of Introductory sociology textbooks that such works tend to misrepresent Merton's theory by favoring one source of strain and ignoring the other. We explain the pattern we have observed in terms of the sociology of knowledge by considering the correspondence of each aspect of the theory with the value commitments of American sociologists.

Some years ago, Merton's theory of anomie (1938) was acclaimed by Cohen (1965:5) as the "most influential single formulation in the sociology of deviance in the last 25 years." More recently, Cole (1975:175) asserted that the original article "has been more frequently cited and reprinted than any other paper in sociology. In undergraduate sociology courses, it is still used as one of the finest examples of sociological theory." These statements are as unchallenged today as when they were made, although as Cole points out, a shift toward the paradigm of labeling theory has taken place in recent years.

In this paper, we consider representations of Merton's theory in introductory textbooks, the inadequacy of these representations,

---

* Previously published in *The American Sociologist* 1979, Vol. 14 (August): 150-156.

and the basis for that inadequacy. As such, this is an exercise in the sociology of sociology. By implication, we raise serious questions about the quality of introductory textbooks currently being published. If such books commonly misrepresent one of the most prominent and "best known" ideas in American sociology, how can other, less prominent ideas be expected to fare? Many students will find in the textbooks their only exposure to important sociological ideas. Even graduate students, we suspect, often gain their first and most enduring impressions from introductory textbooks.[1]

Our argument, in brief, is as follows:

1. Sociologists in America, as Americans, are inclined to seek solutions to social problems within the context of the ideals of the American Way of Life. They also tend to be liberals,[2] and so to seek solutions consistent with the ideology of liberalism in America.
2. The theories that imply such solutions are more likely to be accepted than those that do not.
3. Merton's theory of anomie implies two types of changes as solutions to the "problem" of deviance. One of these is consistent with the ideology of American liberalism, the other is not.
4. We would therefore expect American sociologists who author textbooks to emphasize that aspect of Merton's theory which implies a solution within the framework of American liberal ideology and to ignore that aspect which does not.

Goals, Means and the Integrated Society

Merton's thesis is based on the differential emphasis that societies place on cultural goals and institutional means. For example, some societies emphasize the attainment of cultural goals much more strongly than conformity to the norms prescribing legitimate means. In such societies, efficiency determines the choice of means, and when the limiting case is reached, according to Merton (1957: 133), "any and all procedures which promise attainment of the all-important goal would be permitted." Obviously, the limiting case is rarely reached in human groups. When it is, society as Merton understands it does not exist. There are no legitimate (or illegitimate) means and interaction is characterized by a "war of all against all," the antithesis of society.

At the other extreme is the society that emphasizes institutional means so strongly that the means become ends in themselves, requiring no justification in utilitarian terms. Conformity to them becomes "ritualistic." As might be expected, societies of this type are highly stable and resistant to change. In the short run this may be functional for their maintenance, but in the long run, they may not be flexible enough to adapt to new life conditions.

Between these two extremes, says Merton (1957:134),

> [A]re societies which maintain a rough balance between emphasis upon cultural goals and institutional practices, and these constitute the integrated and relatively stable, though changing societies.

Merton is concerned primarily with societies that emphasize cultural goals over institutional means because (1) the phenomenon of anomie (he argues) is likely to be great in these societies, and (2) he feels that American society approximates the type.

Merton's Two Sources of Strain

To discover the sources of strain leading to deviant behavior, Merton asks two questions: (1) Why are the rates of deviance higher in societies of the American type than in societies of the ritualistic type? And (2) Why, in societies of the American type, are there higher rates of deviance in the lower classes than in the middle and upper classes?

On the first question, Merton argues that the relatively greater stress on goal attainment in societies of the American type weakens the norm prescribing legitimate means:

> With such differential emphases upon goals and institutional procedures, the latter may be so vitiated by the stress on goals as to have the behavior of individuals limited only by considerations of technical expediency. In this context, the sole significant question becomes: Which of the available procedures is more efficient in netting the culturally approved value? The technically most effective procedure, whether culturally legitimate or not, becomes typically preferred

to institutionally prescribed conduct. As the process of attenuation continues, the society becomes unstable and there develops what Durkheim called "anomie" (or normlessness). (Merton 1957:135).

We wish to emphasize several points concerning this source of strain. First, the key variable is the "differential procedures." Second, the strain which it generates may be expect to affect persons at all class levels within the society, the rich as well as the poor, the powerful as well as the powerless.[3] Third, and perhaps most important for our purposes, the factors involved in this source of strain are basic to the American Way of Life. Indeed, America's greatness as a nation is often attributed to this emphasis on goal attainment combined with the competition within a "market."

Thus, if Merton is correct in his reasoning, this source of strain cannot be eliminated or even reduced significantly without making fundamental changes in that way of life. This final point lies at the heart of our explanation for the neglect of this source of strain in introductory sociology texts.

Merton answers the second question—why is there more deviance in the lower than in the upper class in societies of the American type—as follows: If the tendency toward deviance is generally great in societies that emphasize the attainment of cultural goals, then that tendency will be even greater in those classes whose access to legitimate means to these goals is limited. It is the combination of a class structure (which provides unequal access to legitimate means) with an emphasis on goal attainment (which transcends class lines) that explains the higher rates of deviance in the lower classes. Merton (1957:146) makes this point quite explicit:

> It is only when a system of cultural values extols, virtually above all else, certain common success-goals, *for the population at large*, while the social structure rigorously restricts or completely closes access to approved modes of reaching these goals for a *considerable part of the same population* that deviant behavior ensues on a large scale.

If common success goals are taken for granted, the significant factor in this aspect of Merton's thesis is the variation in access to legitimate means or opportunity structures. As we shall see, this fact may be crucial in understanding why this source of strain is dealt with significantly more frequently than the one discussed earlier.

The Findings

We examined the treatment of Merton's theory of anomie in all of the introductory textbooks available to us that were published in the last 15 years.[4] Briefly, what we found was this: Of the 29 books that included a discussion of Merton's thesis, 27 made reference to strains generated by a lack of access to means within the lower classes in societies of the American type. Seven made reference also to strains generated by the emphasis on goals over means in these same societies. Two made reference only to strains generated by the emphasis on goals over means.

The bias is particularly striking in light of the tradition of anomie theory as initiated by Durkheim (1951:241-276), who clearly focused on the goal structure of society as the source of anomie. Anomic suicide is the result of the failure of society to discipline aspirations, too keep goals commensurate with means. Thus, our findings indicate not only a misrepresentation of Merton's formulation of the theory, but a lack of sensitivity to the larger tradition of anomie theory.

Before discussing the social changes implied by Merton's thesis, we wish to eliminate some other possible explanations for the pattern we have observed. First, since both sources of strain are equally structural, the focus on one of them cannot be the result of a preference for structural explanations. Second, some might argue that the emphasis on "differential access to means" is more compatible with the intra-societal, social psychological orientation that has for some years characterized research in the sociology of deviant behavior. However, both aspects of the thesis have given rise to social-psychological questions and research on topics ranging from the perceptions of the adequacy of means (in relations to various goals) to the problem of meaning (see Cole and Zuckerman, 1964a).[5] Third, *both* sources of strain raise questions that lend themselves to or require comparative or historical research. The demanding nature of cross-cultural research may explain some of the reluctance to do research on differential commitment to goals, but research on this subject does not necessarily require cross-national data. Studies on crime rates, for example, could be done within nations (especially highly pluralistic ones) by comparing levels of commitment of regional, ethnic, religious, and other groups. Thus, we believe there is no adequate justification on either theoretical or methodological grounds, or in terms of the demands of contemporary research design and measurement, for emphasizing only one aspect of Merton's theory. We therefore turn our attention to influences beyond the strict limits of sociology itself to explain what we have observed.

Implications for Change

All theories have implications for change as a solution to the "problem conditions" to which they refer. Merton's formulation of the theory of anomie implies that if the structure of American society were altered in certain ways, the strains associated with that structure would be reduced. In turn, other things being equal, one would expect a reduction in deviant adaptations to these strains. In the following discussion, we will not attempt to deal with all of the implications for change which come to mind, but only those which are relevant to our thesis. We will discuss some of the more obvious consequences of these changes, and how they relate to the ideology of American liberalism.

First, strain and deviance, to the degree that they derive from a disproportionate emphasis upon goals, may be reduced by deemphasizing goals (I). This may take the form of a more "integrated" society (I.A.), in which there is a "rough balance between emphasis on cultural goals and institutionalized practices." In such a society people, would get satisfaction from simply participating according to the rules, as well as from attaining goals. Or it may take the form of a ritualistic society (I.B.), in which there is little concern for goal-attainment and almost all satisfactions from participation. "Winning" would have little meaning.

Because of the close functional relationship between goal-attainment and the average level of performance, we would expect a deemphasis on the former to have a depressing effect on the latter. Indeed, if anomie is the cost of a relatively greater emphasis on goal-attainment, then a reduced performance level is the cost of any change in social structure which would produce a more "integrated" (I.A.) society. The impact of such a change would be greatest in the productive (i.e., economic) and education subsystems of our society, although it would be felt in all those subsystems with strong performance orientations. Moreover—and this is a critical consideration—it would affect persons at all class levels, since it involves a change in the general orientation of the society. Translated into economic terms, this change would, other things remaining equal, reduce the growth rate of productivity, since productivity must certainly be highly dependent on the emphasis on quality performance. This would, in turn, reduce the level of material well-being.

Less obvious perhaps, but equally important, is the depressing effect such a change would have on the rate of innovation in American society. Whatever one's concept of moral and economic progress, the ability to innovate is essential to its attainment. Durkheim (1964:70) was particularly concerned with the conditions that facilitate change in the moral norms:

> [I]n order that these transformations [in moral norms] may be possible, the collective sentiments at the basis of mortality must not be hostile to change, and consequently must have moderate energy. If they were too strong, they would no longer be plastic. Every pattern in an obstacle to new patters, to the extent that the first is inflexible.

Thus,

> The authority which the moral conscience enjoys must not be excessive; otherwise no one would dare criticize it, and it would too easily congeal into an immutable form. To make progress, individuality must be able to express itself. In order that the originality of the idealist whose dreams transcend his century may find expression, it is necessary that the originality of the criminal, who is below the level of his time, shall also be possible (1964:71).

It hardly needs to be pointed out that if the "solution" to strain and deviance took the form of a "ritualistic" society (I.B.), all of the consequences we have suggested in connection with an "integrated" society would be dramatically amplified. Further, in America, both solutions (I.A. or I.B.) would be classified as radical, for neither is consistent with the orientation toward performance values and competition which pervades American ideology. We suggest that these implications are what induce textbook authors to ignore this aspect of Merton's thesis.

We now turn to Merton's second source of strain: The disparity between the commitment of lower-class persons to common success goals and their relative lack of access to legitimate means for pursuing these goals (II). Merton's argument implies that strain from this source (and the deviance associated with it) can be decreased either by reducing the commitment of lower-class persons to common success goals (II.A.), or by increasing their access to legitimate means (II.B.), or by some combination of the two.

Again, the first of these moves—reducing the commitment of lower class persons to common success goals (II.A.)—can be expected to reduce the motivation of lower-class persons to succeed and, concommitantly, the quality of their performance. However, it might also be expected to have a similar effect in the higher classes if it results in a decline in the number of lower-class persons who are motivated to compete for cultural goals. In other words, higher-class persons can be expected to be less concerned with performance as their status becomes more secure.

A reduction in commitment to common success goals will also decrease the rate of upward social mobility of lower-class persons. This would in turn reduce the rate at which talent (performance capabilities) within the lower classes is developed and utilized. Some theorists (e.g., Cloward and Oblin, 1960) claim that in societies such as ours the emphasis on competition and on common success goals functions precisely to meet a need for a high level of performance, especially in more technical work roles. Competition, although obviously not without drawbacks, appears to be the most efficient way of allocating persons to work roles by insuring a high degree of correspondence between the demands of the work and the capabilities of the persons being "allocated." Were an industrial society to depend upon a system of ascription based, for exmple, on kinship relationships, the allocation of persons to work roles would be much less efficient. Merely being the child of a lab technician does not qualify one (or make one willing) to be a lab technician.

The second solution to the "problem" of deviance implied by the second part of Merton's thesis is to increase the access of lower-class persons to legitimate means for attaining cultural goals (II.B.). Logically, this solution can take at least two forms: All occupations could be "leveled" by according them equal rewards (II.B.1.), or, unequal rewards could be retained, but the *use* of those rewards could be controlled so that they would not produce unequal opportunity (II.B.2.).

If the reward structure for all occupations were leveled (II.B.1.), inequality of opportunity would certainly be reduced since there would be no inequality in rewards to translate into inequality of opportunity. However, because of the functional significance of inequality in the reward structure for the motivation to performance, it could also be expected to reduce the average level of performance at all class levels. It would also be more difficult to fill top level positions of responsibility since making the sacrifices involved in preparing for them would no longer "pay."

The second of these approaches—retaining inequality in the reward structure but controlling the use of those rewards (II.B.2.)— has two variations. The first and most extreme would require that successful performers be allowed to use their rewards to purchase only consumer goods and services (II.B.2a.). In other words, it would preclude the use of rewards for "investments," which would yield in advantage (in the pursuit of various success goals) without additional effort by the investor. This solution could be implemented in America only by eliminating the private ownership of capital goods and equalizing educational and occupational opportunities. This solution is most consistent with the ideals, if not the actual practices, of many socialist countries, notably the Soviet Union.[6]

The less extreme variant of this approach, which may be called the "Capitalistic-Meritocratic" solution (II.B.2b.), seeks to equalize opportunity without eliminating the private ownership of capital goods. It takes the form of policies designed to increase equality of opportunity in the education and occupational subsystems. Clearly, "Capitalistic-Meritocracy" is an attenuated meritocracy since private ownership does provide some actors with an advantage over others. This, it can only be a partial solution.

It seems clear that of the changes we have discussed, *only those which emphasize the equalization of opportunity while retaining inequality in the distribution of rewards and the private ownership of capital goods would be acceptable within the context of American liberal values.*

Discussion

Americans have often been admonished for placing too much emphasis on "winning" and not enough on "playing the game." From this point of view, the solution to the problem of deviance is to scale down ambition. Why have sociologists not advocated this solution, stressing the central role of goal-attainment in the genesis of deviance in America? We think there are two reasons.

First, this mode of thought is not so characteristic of American liberals as it is of American conservatives. In fact, a deemphasis on winning is often viewed by liberals as merely an ideology propagated by the winners to "cool out" the losers.

Second, we suspect that many of those who advocate a deemphasis on winning do not see the "structure of aspirations" as intrinsic to the American way of life. Social observers trained in fields other than sociology (e.g., conservative literati, journalists, and commentators), may approach the problem in a different way because they are less given than sociologists to an understanding of society as constituted of structural elements systematically related. This last idea is a primary heuristic assumption of sociology and is not so clearly characteristic of other modes of thought.

Conclusion

Our principal concern has been to explain the tendency among professional sociologists to "play down" the aspect of Merton's theory of anomie that relates deviance to the relatively greater emphasis on cultural goals than on institutional means, and to "play up" the aspect that relates deviance in the lower classes to the relative lack of access to legitimate means available for pursuing cultural goals. Our explanation, in general terms, is that both tendencies are a function of "evaluative" rather than scientific considerations (Parsons, 1951:330). We argue that the commitments of American sociologists to the basic features of the American Way of Life and beyond that to the positive functional significance of that Way for the attainment of cultural goals may be responsible for their tendency to amplify one aspect of Merton's thesis and to give diminished attention to the other. [7]

Their commitments have led sociologists to emphasize the aspect that appears to promise a solution within the context of American liberal values, and to deemphasize the aspect that does not.

We would like to make it clear that we are not suggesting, even by implication, that any less attention should be given to the evaluation of theories in terms of the traditional canons of science, for example, internal consistency or correspondence with fact. We do suggest that sociology can profit a great deal from a conscious effort to analyze theoretical developments (or the lack of them) in terms of the possible effects of what we have called evaluative considerations.

References

Cloward, Richard and Lloyd Ohlin
    1960 *Delinquency and Opportunity,* New York: The Free Press
Cohen, Albert
    1965 "The sociology of the deviant act: Anomie theory and beyond,"
    American Sociological Review, 30:5-14.

Cole, Stephen
   1975 "The growth of scientific knowledge: Theories of deviance as a case study." pp. 175-219 in L. Coser (ed.). *The idea of Social Structure: Papers in Honor of Robert K. Merton.* New York: Harcourt Brace Jovanovich.
Cole, Stephen and H. Zuckerman
   1964a "Inventory of empirical studies." pp. 243-289 in M. Clinard (ed.), *Anomie and Deviant Behavior.* New York: The Free Press
   1964b "Annotated bibliography of theoretical studies." pp. 290-311 in M. Clinard (ed.), *Anomie and Deviant Behavior.* New York: The Free Press.
Durkheim, Emile
   1951 *Suicide: A Study in Sociology,* New York: The Free Press.
   1964 *The Rules of Sociological Method.* New York: The Free Press.
Gouldner, Alvin
   1973 *Foreword.* pp. ix-xiv in Ian Taylor, Paul Walton, and Jock Young, *The New Criminology,* New York: Harper and Row.
Hilbert, R.E.
   1976 "The theory of anomie as an explanation for deviance in America." pp. 129-160 in Taylor and White (eds.). *Issues and Ideas: 1776-1976.* Norman, OK: University of Oklahoma Press.
Lipset, Seymour Martin and Everett C. Ladd, Jr.
   1972 "The politics of American sociologists." *American Journal of Sociology* 78:67-104.
Merton, Robert K.
   1957 "Social structure and anomie." pp. 131-[1938] *160 in Social Theory and Social Structure.* New York: The Free Press.
Parsons, Talcott
   1951 *The Social System.* New York: The Free Press.
Srole, Leo
   1956 *"Social integration and certain corollaries: An exploratory study."* *American Sociological Review 21:*709-716.
Wright, Charles W.
   1976 *Theoretical Constructions of Deviance Within Society: The Heretic and the Infidel.* University of Notre Dame, PhD Dissertation.
Wright, Charles W. and R. E. Hilbert
   1978 *"Value implications of the functional theory of deviance."* Paper presented at the Midwestern Sociological Meetings, Omaha.

End Notes

1. We do not claim to shed any light on how professional sociologists "understand" Merton's theory, nor that the authors of introductory texts understand the theory as the present it. However, we have spent most of our careers as specialist in the sociology of deviant behavior, and we are prepared to speculate that the "understanding" reflected in the textbooks corresponds closely with more scholarly renditions of Merton's work.

2. Lipset and Ladd (1972) clearly document the suggestion that most American sociologists are liberals. More precisely, they content that American sociologists are inclined to support those democratic party presidential nominees who lean farthest to the left. For example, "In 1968, a larger proportion of sociologists that of any other discipline preferred McCarthy (66%) to Humphrey for the democratic nomination" (1972:87). At the same time, few American sociologists are radicals; most appear to be relatively comfortable within the framework of the American two party system. But depending upon the time, the issues, and the availability of options, five to ten percent of the members of the discipline express dissatisfaction with the offerings of the major parties and support left wing third parties and candidates.

3. A substantial portion of Merton's discussion of "innovation" as an adaptation to structural strain deals with middle and upper class behavior.

4. We do not know what percentage of all introductory textbooks are included in our survey; however, we think it is sizable. In any case, we see no reason to believe that those books which were not included are substantially different from those we examined in their treated of Merton's thesis. Thus, at this time we feel the assumption that our sample is representative would be as difficult to challenge as to defend. An appendix containing an annotated bibliography of the works examined will be provided upon request.

    In our figures, we did not include those texts which made no reference to Merton's statements on anomie. Most notable of those is the widely used sixth edition of Broom and Selznik.

    Later we plan to examine systematically the more sophisticated treatments of the subject in social problems and crime and delinquency texts. Preliminary findings suggest that Merton's thesis is represented in much the same way in these texts.

5. In this regard, there are a number of conceptual developments which individualize the concept of anomie, e.g., Srole's (1956) "anomia" and various derivations of the concept of alienation. Many of these developments focus on the actor's orientation to goals (see, e.g., Cole and Zuckerman, 1964b).

6. Some quasi-leftists such as Gouldner (1973) have seen Merton's theory as offering an "incisive critique" of American social structure; however, most radical sociologists are not receptive to Merton's work. Although we have

no carefully surveyed treatments of Merton's theory in "radical" or conflict-oriented textbooks as opposed to the more "conventional" ones, our general impression is that it is more often than not ignored in such texts. The reason for this is not entirely clear, but in fact the broader system of Merton's thought does not lend itself to radical interpretation (see Wright and Hilbert, 1978).

7. It could be argued that a less elaborate but equally plausible explanation for what we observed is that sociologists are simply ignorant of the complexity of Merton's theory. This may indeed be part of the explanation, but it seems unlikely to be the major part. After all, Merton's theory, by all accounts, is one of the most prominent and "best known" theories in the literature. It therefore seems more reasonable to argue that the bias is positively motivated and not merely the result of ignorance.

Contrasting Conceptions of Deviance in Sociology: Functionalism and Labeling Theory

Charles W. Wright & Susan C. Randall

The proponents of different theories are like the members of different language-culture communities." (Kuhn, 1970, p. 205). The controversy between the anomie and labeling theories of deviant behavior is likened to what Kuhn (1970) terms a "communication breakdown." This lack of communication is traced to three fundamental differences between the general paradigms on which the theories of deviance rest—etiological functionalism and interactionism respectively. These basic differences, and their implications, are analyzed with an eye to facilitating what Kuhn (1970) refers to as the process of "translation" between "seemingly incommensurable universes of discourse."

During the last decade there has been a debate among sociologists concerning the relative merits of the functional and labeling perspectives on deviant behavior. Unfortunately, many of the assertions, charges and countercharges emanating from these two theoretical camps have been guided more by an interest

---

This paper is a revised version of one presented at the Annual Meeting of the Society for the Study of Social Problems, New York City, August 1976, and subsequently published in *The British Journal of Criminology*, V. 18 (3) (1978): 217-31.

in enhancing the position of a particular theoretical stance than by a desire to analyze objectively the basic elements of conceptualization which distinguish them. This lack of attention to the underlying points of difference in the approaches has generated considerable confusion in the dispute, often resulting in proponents of the functionalist and labeling perspectives talking past, rather than to, one another.

As sociologists who see considerable value in the distinctive contributions of both of these approaches to the analysis of deviance, we have undertaken in this paper the task of pinpointing the major assumptions and sources of difference between the functional and labeling perspectives. Lest the reader dismiss this as merely another attempt to extol the virtues of one and denounce the vices of the other, let us hasten to add that this is not our intention. Rather, we seek to lay the groundwork for a more precise understanding of both perspectives in the hope that this may reduce the confusion surrounding their respective claims. We do not, however, herein attempt a synthesis of the functionalist and labeling approaches. Indeed, the two perspectives may well represent incommensurable universes of discourse such that no synthesis is feasible. The possibility of unification requires, as a minimum, the sharing of certain basic assumptions about the social world. As will be illustrated in this paper, the functionalist and labeling perspectives diverge on so many essential elements of definition and conceptualization that they may indeed represent two entirely different "disciplinary matrices" (as Kuhn, 1970, Postscript, uses that term). The differences between the two systems of thought may be so vast as not only to render synthesis problematic but to undermine as well the suggestion that there has been an historical accumulation of knowledge in the area of the sociology of deviance. For example, can the new perspective which currently dominates the sociology of deviance be said to have "built on" the historical achievements and/or failings of the functionalist analysis of deviance? Can it be claimed that the recent developments (i.e., in the last few decades) of theory in the sociology of deviance fit the ideal of "scientific progress," i.e., a progressively more refined knowledge of some external reality rooted in the work of predecessors? Such questions are implicit throughout this analysis. In order to shed light on them, as well as to accomplish our primary goal of clarification of the dispute, we will concern ourselves with an elucidation of the primary points of *divergence* (a task which we see as a necessary first step before analysis of any possible areas of compatibility may be fruitfully undertaken).

In this analysis, we are likening the current functionalist-labeling dispute to what Kuhn (1970) refers to as a "communication breakdown" between the adherents of different paradigms.

> Two men who perceive the same situation differently, but nevertheless employ the same vocabulary in its discussion, must be using words differently. They speak, that is, from what I have called incommensurable viewpoints....Such problems, though they first become evident in communication, are merely linguistic, and they cannot be resolved simply by stipulating the definitions of troublesome terms.... They cannot, that is, resort to a neutral language which both use in the same way and which is adequate to the statement of both their theories or even of both those theories' empirical consequences.... Briefly put, what the participants in a communication breakdown *can* do is recognize each other as members of different language communities, and then become translators. Taking the difference between their own intra- and inter-group discourse as *itself a subject for study*, they can first attempt to discover the terms and locutions that, used unproblematically within each community, are nevertheless foci for trouble for inter-group discussions." (Kuhn, 1970, pp. 200-202) (emphasis added).

For heuristic purposes, we will concentrate on the most disparate features of the approaches which we view as the primary sources of confusion and major obstacles to communication. In this effort, we will be principally concerned with contrasting basic elements of the general perspectives rather than with systematically reviewing the works of all the important theorists. Our depiction of "the" functionalist and labeling perspectives, then, will not mirror precisely the formulations of all their various authors; rather, we will focus on key elements abstracted from certain of those formulations in an attempt to clarify differences in basic assumptions which underlie the two schools.

Functionalism and Labeling: Deviance Causation vs. Deviance Creation

Our comparison of the functionalist and labeling approaches to deviance will focus on what we believe to be the three primary sources of disagreement between them: (a) the temporal element involved in the conceptualization of deviance, i.e., the time relation seen to exist between "rule existence" and "behavioral violation"; (b) the important, but seldom recognized, difference between a "norm" and a "rule" (based on a more general conceptual divergence concerning the character of social life); and (c) the issue of whether or not there is a qualitative difference between deviant and non-deviant acts, requiring a special theory of the deviant act.

The temporal sequence

The type of confusion and lack of communication which characterizes much of the functionalist vs. labeling theory debate is typified by Merton's response to the now famous statement made by Becker (1963, p. 9) in his *Outsiders*: *"(S)ocial groups create deviance by making the rules whose infraction constitutes deviance*, and by applying those rules to particular people and labeling them outsiders." Merton (1971, p. 827) retorts that this theoretical claim "is blatantly true and trivial: namely the statement that behavior cannot be considered 'deviant' unless there are social norms from which that behavior departs. It seems banal and safe to stipulate: no rule, no rule violating behavior" (emphasis added). At first glance, Merton's sharp criticism may seem warranted. However, we think that his response indicates that he is missing the essential feature of Becker's point of view. Further, we contend that this misunderstanding arises out of the difference in time sequence underlying Merton's and Becker's perspectives on the relationship between (a) the existence of a rule and (b) the occurrence of behavior which is conceived as violating that rule.

The entire functionalist approach to deviance rests on the assumption that the rule (or, more correctly, the norm) comes *first*, then the violation of it. The general theoretical stance of the functionalists requires that a norm be viewed as existing (in the institutional milieu and the orientation of the actor) *prior* to behavior which can be said to deviate from it. However, the labelists assume exactly the opposite time sequence: Behavior occurs and then (perhaps) a rule is invoked and the behavior is reacted to as deviant. That is, action which *eventually* comes to be viewed as violative may well *precede* the existence or application of rules which *eventually* come to prohibit it. As Becker (1963, p. 134) points out: "A rule may be drawn up simply to serve someone's special interest and a rationale for it later found in some general value. In the same way, a spontaneous act of enforcement may be legitimized by creating a rule to which it can be related" (emphasis added). Even in the case of what might be seen by some as a "pre-existing rule" (e.g., a law), it cannot be known *prior to reaction* whether a given rule will be seen as applicable to given behavior. That is, whether an act will be reacted to as "rule violative," giving rise to deviance, cannot be known prior to the concrete interaction situation. We shall return to this point shortly. However, before exploring further implications of the temporal element for the two perspectives, we must first turn to the real source of the disagreement—the distinction between a "norm" and a "rule" and, more generally, between the functionalist and interactionist views of social life.

Norms vs. rules

(1) The normative view of deviation

Within the functionalist perspective, individual deviance and conformity are always defined with reference to "institutionalized norms." Norms provide the patterns for human conduct; institutionalized norms are shared, i.e., relatively "fixed" guides for interaction which govern social life and make it somewhat stable and predictable. These are transmitted to neophytes via the socialization process and are internalized by group members, who thus develop a *commitment* to these "interiorized common ways of life." Socialization and internalization then provide the basis for coordinated social interaction based on the sharing of commitments, understandings and behavioral expectations among the members of a society. Deviance represents both the violation of a *shared* understanding and the violation of a norm to which the *actor* is/has been oriented and committed.

The central question for the functionalist theory of deviance is to explain why an actor would violate a norm to which he has been committed. The exact answer varies from one theorist to another but, in essence, they agree that deviance occurs when an actor is placed in a "moral bind" by the social system(s) of which he is a member. That is, deviance occurs when the system is disequilibrated in such a manner that the actor is placed under pressure or strain which *forces* him to violate one set of normative expectations or another. The quintessential illustration of this type of explanation is provided by Merton's theory of social structure and anomie (1938). Here, the actor is *originally* committed *both* to attaining the culturally favored goals and to doing so by the use of legitimate means. However, because of socially structured barriers to the use of legitimate means characteristic of certain sectors of the American class structure, some actors are put in a "moral bind." That is, some are unable both to strive for the goals and utilize legitimate means to do so—they must give up one or the other (or both, as in the case of the retreatist). Thus, the lack of integration of the system forces them into deviance, i.e., forces them to breach one or both sets of commitments.

Deviance, then, is problem-solving behavior, an adaption to strain imposed on an actor who is structurally prevented from fulfilling all of the normative commitments incumbent upon him as a *member* of the society. Deviance, from the functionalist perspective, is *constituted by the act* of violating a pre-existing normative commitment, a shared understanding. If there is no shared, *pre-existing* norm governing an action or if the actor is unaware of, or uncommitted to, that norm, (e.g., if he were never committed to the goals or means in the first place), no "*deviance*" can occur, regardless of the legal status of the action or the extent of reaction. "'Conformity' and 'deviation,' in the present context, have meaning only in relation to the fact that the actors in social systems are oriented to social norms that are internalized as part of their personality" (Johnson, 1960, p. 552). Thus, if a child were reared in a criminal subculture and came to internalize norms requiring criminal conduct, such conduct could not, from this perspective, be termed "deviant." However, if he were to "go straight," this would fall within the functionalists' theoretical conception of deviance.

In sum, from the functionalist perspective, deviant behavior is viewed as a failure to live up to norms that are institutionalized in a society. Moreover, it is the failure to conform on the part of a certain category of persons—those who are "members" of that society. If the failure to abide by the norms is that of one who has not been socialized into the pattern, (e.g., the stranger, the outsider or the "psychopath") or one who is incapable of receiving such socialization (e.g., the "idiot"), the behavior is not of interest from this point of view. That is, the behavior is not "deviant." The functionalist problem of deviant behavior involves action carried out by an actor who, once having been committed to the norms, has withdrawn that commitment. Thus, the paramount question for such theorists is: "What are the forces which may act to overcome a member's commitment to the dominant order and lead him to violate norms once cherished?"

(2) The time element in functionalist-anomie theory

As we have just discussed, the functionalist perspective *requires* that norms precede deviance, and that deviance is established by norm violation, independently of reaction. The time sequence and model of deviance causation employed by these theorists can be illustrated as in Figure 1.

Functionalists assume that if the actor's problem-solving response is perceived by others as violating the norm which they

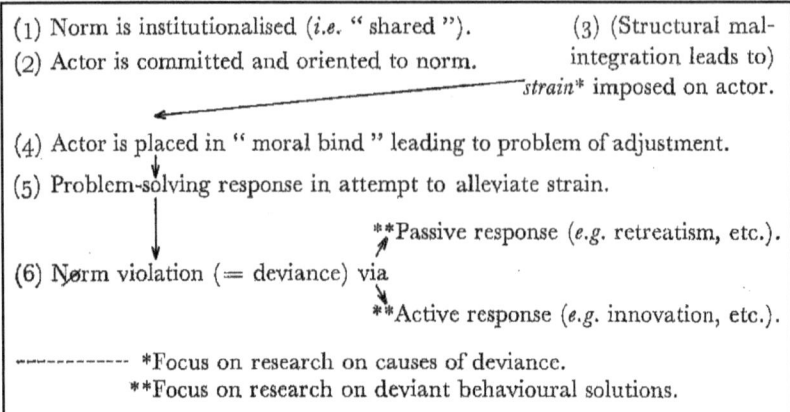

Figure 1. Time Sequence in Functionalist Model of Deviance Causation

share with the actor, they will negatively sanction him. However, even if the actor were not apprehended, (i.e., were able to keep his deviance secret) or if he were able to work out a solution which would not evoke a negative reaction (e.g., withdrawal into the sick role), or if his deviance was overlooked (e.g., due to power differentials, etc.), he would *still be deviant* because he has violated his normative commitment. This is so because the concept of institutionalized norms provides a relatively stable, fixed starting-point for analysis from which functionalists can talk about deviance *independently* of reaction.

In short, when Merton says "of course" social groups create deviance by making rules, he means "of course," from his theoretical vantage point, *norms* must be conceptualized as existing prior to an act which is viewed as being in violation of them. However, as we shall see in the next section, Becker intended something quite different by his statement.

(3) An interactionist view of deviance creation

"It is the social process in group life that creates and upholds rules, not the rules that create and uphold group life" (Blumer, 1969, p. 19). For the labelists, the social world is not as eminently predictable as it is for the functionalists. The form and substance of interaction is not guided by norms or stable shared understandings. The structure of an interaction situation and the rules that will govern behavior in that situation are developed in interaction. As Blumer (1969, p. 18) says: "Most sociological schemes rest on the belief that a human society exists in the form of an established order of living, with that order resolvable into adherence to sets of rules, norms, values, and sanctions that specify to people how they are to act in their different situations ... First, it is just not true that the full expanse of life in a human society, in any human society, is but an expression of pre-established forms of joint action ... Second, we have to recognize that even in the case of pre-established and repetitive joint action *each instance* of such joint action is just as much a result of an interpretative process as is a new form of joint action..." (emphasis added).

Unlike institutionalized *norms*, *rules* are not "fixed" or stable; they are in (or are subject to) flux, open to interpretation, negotiation and modification. And, unlike a definitive quality of institutionalized norms, rules *need not be shared*; rules may be *imposed* on an actor who is not committed to them or perhaps not even aware of their existence. Because interaction is not viewed as governed by stable behavioral guidelines, we cannot know the character or outcome of an interaction situation prior to the interaction taking place. The importance of such a perspective for the study of deviance lies in the implication that "what the rules are" is established only in the *immediate* context of interaction; hence, what will be considered deviant or conformative can only be established *via reaction*. The labeling perspective thus adopts Mead's social behaviorist stance: We can only know the significance of our gestures via the behavioral reaction of others. The meaning of an act is contingent upon audience interpretation of it (see Mead, 1934: Part I). Thus, whether or not a given action will be reacted to as "rule violative," giving rise to deviance, cannot be known prior to reaction. From the labeling perspective, deviance is *constituted by reaction* to the behavior as deviant—*not* by the behavior itself. Hence, deviance is not an act; it is an *interactive relationship*.

(4) The time element in labeling analysis

In the functional approach the norm ("shared pattern") is always presumed to precede the act from which it deviates; in labeling analysis the opposite time sequence is implied. Deviance is created only *after* behavior occurs, at which time a rule is invoked or imposed on that behavior, defining it as deviant. The time sequence and model of deviance creation employed by labeling theory can be diagrammed as follows:

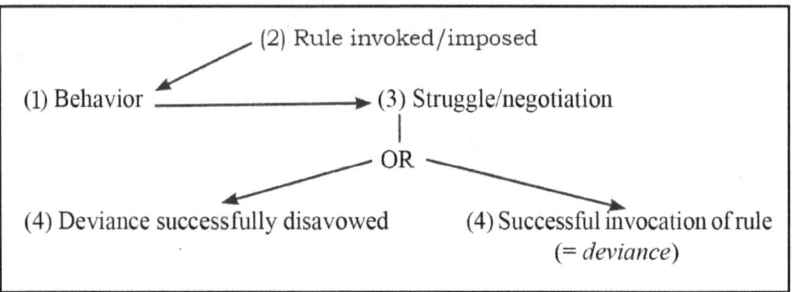

Figure 2. Time Sequence in Labeling Model of Deviance Creation

This suggestion, that the rule comes, analytically, *after* the behavior occurs rather than (pre)existing" as a norm to be departed from" has a number of ramifications for the conceptualization of deviance. For one thing, the actor not sharing a rule may not even know of its existence; hence, the behavior he commits is not, *from his perspective*, violation.[53] Secondly, unlike a norm, the rule need not be viewed as existing prior to the "violative" pattern of action. A *rule* may be applied ex post facto, whereas the notion of ex post facto application of norms is a contradiction in terms. A further implication which really lies at the heart of the theoretical difference, is that rules, not being shared, need not be taken as stable elements guiding human relations. As a result, the situation and the whole interaction process is regarded as (at least) in flux, perhaps (at most) totally unspecified as to behavioral expectations for one or both of the parties to the interaction. In a world populated by "rules" rather than "norms" the reaction to an act is not so eminently predictable as imagined above (see pp. 220-22). One final, but very important, implication of this conceptualization of deviance should be noted here. Because deviance is constituted by reaction rather than behavior, no *actual* behavior need occur in order for deviance to be created. Behavior may simply be imputed and followed by reaction. Thus, if someone is believed to be a "child molester," the consequences of that label will exist regardless of the "truth value" of the charge.[54] Similarly, if "unapprehended rule violations" occur, they do not constitute "deviance."[55] In a sense, then rule violative *behavior* is irrelevant to the labelist's conception of deviance; it is the *reaction* which counts."[56] Note, for example, the following formulations by prominent labeling theorists:

> Deviance is not a property *inherent* in certain forms of behavior; it is a property *conferred upon* these forms by the audiences which directly or indirectly witness them.... (I)t is the audience which eventually decides whether or not any given action or actions will become a visible case of deviation (Erickson, 1962, p. 308).

And,

> Forms of behavior per se do not differentiate deviants from non-deviants; it is the responses of the conventional and conforming members of the society who identify and interpret behavior as deviant which sociologically transform persons into deviant. (Kitsuse, 1962, p. 253).

For the functionalist, in contrast, norm-violative *behavior* is essential; concrete *reaction* by others is irrelevant. Within the functionalist framework, an actor may violate a norm to which he is committed and, possessed of conscience, feel guilt over the violation, and perhaps even come to view himself as " deviant" in the absence of any negative reaction (real or feared) by others.

The difference between the time sequences implied by the functionalist and labeling perspectives can be further illustrated with two concepts drawn from Matza's (1969) important discussion of how one "becomes deviant." The first is "guilt," a concept of which Matza makes little, explicitly, but which forms the primary underpinning of a large portion of his treatise. For Matza, guilt is at the heart of the process of becoming deviant. The second concept, "ban," involves a consideration of how ban morally transforms activity. For Matza, only through an understanding of the means by which both the activity in which the actor is engaged and the actor himself are "made guilty" can we grasp the concept of deviance.

(a) The concept of guilt

There are at least two ways in which the concept of guilt is widely employed. The first we shall refer to as *legal guilt*, the second *psychological guilt*.[57] In the first case, it is possible to speak of the actor being *found* guilty (by others) and being, therefore, in a sense, *made guilty*.[58] In the case of psychological guilt, the actor we may say simply *is* guilty or *feels* guilty in the sense that *he* is disturbed by his action. Legal guilt may be seen as corresponding to the labelists' conception of deviance; psychological guilt to the functionalists.

These two conceptualizations of guilt imply, of course, two wholly separate circumstances concerning the relation of the actor to his action and the patterns which he violates. In the first case, "legal guilt," the actor and the rule may be, in a sense, completely removed from one another. That is, at a point in time the actor may not even know of the rule, nor is the rule necessarily applied to the actor. However, these separate entities may be brought together when, perhaps with no behavioral change on the actor's part, he is placed under the jurisdiction of the rule. In such a case the actor's affiliation with the behavior in question may have originally been "innocent" (i.e., the actor may not even have been cognizant of rules prohibiting the behavior), but the behavior can be, through being brought under the jurisdiction of the rule, "made guilty."

Bringing the actor under the jurisdiction of the rule need not imply that the actor in any sense absorbs the rule, i.e., believes in it. The suggestion is only that the rule now exists in the actor's milieu. Now, the rule is, in Parson's terms (1951), a *condition* of the actor's action. Such is the significance, as we shall see, of being under the jurisdiction of ban. The second conception of guilt, "psychological guilt," implies, of course, a wholly different relation between the actor and the patterns violated. In this case, the actor and the rules are "together" (i.e., as in the Freudian and Parsonian sense, that the rules are literally constituents of the actor's personality). The actor is not necessarily made guilty in that he is brought under the jurisdiction of the rules but "feels guilty" in that he has done something he thinks he should not have done. In Parsonian terms, the rules, rather than being part of the conditions of action (in the situation) are part of the actor's *orientation* to the situation. The actor carried the rules into the situation—they are not imposed by his simply being within their jurisdiction. The actor is not "made guilty" after the fact; rather he himself attaches significance to the action and feels guilty in his own terms.

(b) Ban: the moral transformation of activity

When Matza suggests the existence of guilt, it is clear that he intends something similar to what we have called legal guilt. This stands out in his discussion of ban (as in his discussion of bedevilment, transparency, and apprehension). It is via these processes that the actor is made guilty ex post facto and eventually becomes deviant, i.e., develops a deviant identity. Matza leaves little doubt as to the importance of the illegality of action[59] in the eventual establishment of guilt and of what he means by deviance. Action is *made guilty* and *made deviant* by the fact that it is banned.

> Marijuana use as described there (earlier in the text) was more or less *innocent*. Before considering anything else, I must elaborate, for in truth the marijuana user is already guilty, though only in a certain sense. To make that correction we turn to the first element of signification—ban and its meaning (Matza, 1969, p. 145).

It is ban and simply ban that *first* makes activity guilty. And, as Matza (1969, p. 146) says, this should come as no surprise for this is widely known to be the purpose and consequence of ban. "The moral transformation of activity is the purpose of ban;

the simplest way of summarizing the legislative and purportedly public intention is to predict that *with time* the activity will exist in guilt" (emphasis added).

This statement is consistent with the conception of deviance held by other labelists. It suggests the same time sequence between activity and the relevance of the rule as we have seen in Becker's work. The actor is, at first, innocent. Something then intrudes—the State—which has the power to transform morally the activity, i.e., to change him. Further, the relation between activity and guilt flows in the same time sequence. First, there is innocent activity, later the actor is made to feel guilty: "with time the activity will exist in guilt" (Matza, 1969, p. 146). Legal guilt implies that it is others (those represented and representing the State) who, through ban and reaction, bring the actor and rule together. In initiating the interaction with the rule-violator, the reactor "transforms" innocent activity into guilty activity. Hence, in the process of interaction, initiated and controlled by the State, deviance is created.

Is Deviance To Be Conceived as Qualitatively Different from Conformity?

(1) The labeling perspective

"From this point of view, deviance is *not a quality of the act* the person commits, but rather a consequence of the application by others of rules and sanctions to an 'offender'" (Becker, 1963, p. 9) (emphasis added).[60] Within the labeling perspective no qualitative difference between deviant and conforming behavior need be imputed. The character of *reaction* to the behavior is the only feature which distinguishes the two. Becker's (1963) favorite illustration of this point is the use of marijuana—an ongoing, "innocent" pattern of action which preceded the making of a rule prohibiting such action. Prior to the Federal Bureau of Narcotics' formulation and enforcement of a rule making marijuana use "deviant," Becker (1973, p. 135) says the activity had gone on for years, largely ignored and certainly not regarded by federal officials as "rule violative." From his perspective, the act of smoking marijuana did not shift from conformative to deviant; rather, the official definition and reaction did. We need not assume that the construction of the act by the actor has in any sense undergone modification because of a change in response to it. The act is still an outcome of the same processes as it was before the emergence of the response to it as "deviant." There is no basis for suggesting that the *quality of the act* changes even though the *situation of activity* does, requiring the actor to take the implications of" ban" into account. Hence, the sense is established in which the act is viewed as qualitatively the same before and after rule construction and enforcement. The act is the same; only the reaction to the act has changed. Being reacted to as deviant is the *only sense* in which the act is deviant—it has nothing to do with the character of the act itself.

The bearing of the above on the importance of the question of the etiology of deviant acts should be obvious. If deviant acts are not qualitatively different from other acts, there is no question of the "special etiology" of deviant behavior. This does not necessarily suggest that one need not consider the question of the etiology of acts at all[61] but it does imply that one's conclusions will specify nothing peculiar about the emergence of acts which violate rules as opposed to those which conform to the rules. In short, there is no need for sociologists interested in deviance to develop a special theory of the etiology of deviant acts. Partially as a result of this conclusion, labeling theorists have not been particularly interested in etiological questions, preferring to concentrate their efforts on the interaction among "rule violators" and "rule enforcers." Additionally, the importance of the question of the etiology of rule-breaking acts is diminished in significance simply because deviance as so defined does not necessitate the *existence* of such behavior. That is, application of rules need not be stimulated by an act which violates a rule. Hence, violations and their etiology are relatively insignificant to the perspective.

(2) The functionalist perspective

In contrast to the labelists' stance, the existence of a qualitative difference between deviance and conformity is a central tenet for functionalist theory. Deviance and conformity involve different types of *motivation* and arise from different social-structural features; hence, different explanations are required for each. The source of conformity is to be found in socialization and the internalization of institutionalized patterns as part of the individual's need dispositions. As long as the various sub-systems within which the individual interacts are equilibrated internally and integrated externally, he may be expected to conform to his normative commitments. Deviance, on the other hand, involves (a) the violation of the institutionalized norms of the group, (b) by an actor who is viewed as once having been committed to these patterns. Moreover, the deviant act is characterized by a unique motivational pattern—one which involves the withdrawal of allegiance from, or a compulsive orientation in relation to, valued commitments. Hence, functionalists associate such concepts as "ambivalence" (Parsons, 1951, Chap. 7; Cohen, 1955, Chap. 5; Merton, 1968, pp. 136f); "alienation" (Cloward and Ohlin, 1960, Chap. 2); and "psychological guilt" with deviant acts. It should be noted that, from the labeling perspective, none of these concepts or the change in the actor's orientation which they imply come into play. The actor, being an "outsider" in the first place, is, as Matza indicates, "innocent" in the first place (Matza, 1969, p. 148). Deviance, from the labeling perspective, then raises no problems associated with the processes of withdrawal of legitimacy from a set of pre-existing patterns. On the other hand, this is a primary focus of consideration from the perspective of the functional conceptualization of deviance.

Conclusion

We have attempted to show that much of the confusion characteristic of the labeling vs. functionalist debate arises out of the fact that what is "deviance" to one may or may not be "deviance" to another. Starting from very different assumptions about the character of social life, the two perspectives arrive at very different conceptions regarding what constitutes deviant behavior. As we indicated earlier, no attempt will be made here to present a synthesis of these two theories. However, we hope that, by pointing out some of the major areas of confusion, we have laid the groundwork for better understanding the relation between these approaches. It may be that no real theoretical convergence between the two perspectives is possible. Any attempt at merging these two paradigms would entail large concessions on both sides, not only as to the nature of the phenomenon to be studied, but also as to the character of social life itself. Certainly, any possible synthesis would require much more than the overly simplistic suggestion made by Gibbs and Erickson:

> The issue can be resolved quickly by two admonitions: (1) Normativists (functionalists) cease presuming that data on deviance can be interpreted independently of reactions to deviance; and (2) Reactivists (labelists), cease presuming that reactions to deviance have nothing to do with prior behavior (Gibbs and Erickson, 1975, p. 39).

Despite the vast differences, however, we would like to suggest that future efforts at communication between, if not synthesis of, the two schools might be facilitated by further attention to the process of "translation" suggested by Kuhn (1970, pp. 202-203). Although this process was barely begun in this paper, we hope that the ideas suggested will serve as a step in breaking down the barriers between these seemingly incommensurable universes of discourse.

References

BECKER, H. (1963). *Outsiders.* New York: The Free Press,

BECKER, H. (1973). *Outsiders.* (2nd ed.), New York: The Free Press.

CHAMBLISS, W. (1975). "Functional and conflict theories of crime." New York: MSS Modular Publications, *Module* 17: 1-23.

CLOWARD, R. AND OHLIN L. (1960), *Delinquency and Opportunity.* New York: The Free Press.

COHEN, A. (1955). *Delinquent Boys.* New York: The Free Press.

ERICKSON, K. (1962). "Notes on the sociology of deviance." *Social Problems, 9*, 307-314.

GIBBS, J. (1966). "Conceptions of deviant behavior: the old and the new." *Pacific Sociological Review*, 9, 9-14.

GIBBS, J. (1972), "Issues in defining deviant behavior." In *Theoretical Perspectives on Deviance*, Robert Scott and Jack Douglas, eds. New York: Basic Books, Inc.

GIBBS, J. AND ERICKSON, M. (1975). "Major developments in the sociological study of deviance," *Annual Review of Sociology*, Vol. 1, Alex Inkeles, J. Coleman and Neil Smelser, eds. Palo Alto, California: Annual Reviews, Inc,

HAWKINS, R. AND TIEDMAN, G. (1975). *The Creation of Deviance*. Columbus, Ohio: Charles E. Merrill.

JOHNSON, H. (1960). *Sociology: A Systematic Introduction*. New York: Harcourt Brace and Company.

KATZ, J. (1972). "Deviance, charisma, and rule defined behavior," *Social Problems, 2*:0, 186-202.

KITSUSE, J. (1962). "Societal reactions to deviant behavior: problems of theory and method." *Social Problems*, 9, 247-56.

KUHN, T. (1970). *The Structure of Scientific Revolutions*. Chicago: University of Chicago Press.

LEMERT, E. (1951). *Social Pathology*, New York: McGraw-Hill Co.

LEMERT, E. (1972). *Human Deviance, Social Problems, and Social Control* (2nd ed.), Englewood Cliffs, New Jersey: Prentice-Hall, Inc.

LEMERT, E. (1974). "Beyond Mead: The societal reaction to deviance," *Social Problems*, 21, 457-468.

LEVY, M. J. (1952). *The Structure of Society*. Princeton, New Jersey: Princeton University Press.

MATZA, D. (1969). *Becoming Deviant*. Englewood Cliffs, New Jersey: Prentice-Hall.

MERTON, R. (1968). "Social structure and anomie." *Social Theory and Social Structure*. New York: The Free Press.

MERTON, R. AND NISBET, R. (1971). *Contemporary Social Problems*. New York: Harcourt Brace Javonovich.

PARSONS, T. (1937). *The Structure of Social Action*. New York: McGraw-Hill Book Co.

PARSONS, T. (1951). *The Social System*. New York: The Free Press.

POLLNER, M. (Ig74-). "Sociological and commonsense models of the labeling process." In *Ethnomethodology*, Roy Turner, ed. Harmondsworth, England: Penguin Books.

QUINNEY, R. (1965). "Is criminal behaviour deviant behaviour?" *Brit.J. Criminol.* 5, 132-142.

RAINS, P. (1975). "Imputations of deviance: a retrospective essay on the labeling prospective." *Social Problems*, 23, I-II.

SCHUR, E. (1971). *Labeling Deviant Behavior*. New York: Harper and Row,

TAYLOR, I., WALTON, P. AND YOUNG J. (1973). *The New Criminology.* New York, Harper and Row.

End Notes

1. The dispute has also been carried on under such headings as "normative vs. reactive" (Gibbs, 1972, 1975), "normative vs. interpretive" (Hawkins and Tiedeman, 1975), etc.

2. Indeed this may account for the failure of the few attempts at suggesting possible lines of synthesis (e.g., Schur, 1971, pp. 138-48; Gibbs and Erickson, 1975, pp. 39-40; Hawkins and Tiedeman, 1975, pp, 12-15) to generate any new, systematic blending of the two perspectives.

3. Such a suggestion is at least implicit in the writings of Matza (1969, Part I) and Schur (1971, pp. 136-48).

4. However, we will draw heavily upon the formulations of Merton (1968, 1971) and Becker (1963, 1973) whom we view as the most influential contemporary representatives of the anomie functionalist and labeling traditions, respectively. Some readers may find it curious that in relation to labeling theory we take as paradigmatic the work of Becker (1963) rather than that of Lemert (1951). We would contend that there are important differences between the perspectives of these two scholars and that, in the light of the direction in which labeling theory has developed, it is Becker's rather than Lemert's work which has had the greater influence. Despite what the chronology of their writings would suggest, we believe that both historically and theoretically Becker's work "established" labeling theory. This is not to say that Lemert's early writings had no influence. Rather, the suggestion is that widespread recognition of the similarity between Lemert's Social Pathology (1951) and the developing labeling perspective came after the publication of Becker's Outsiders (1963) resulted in widespread scholarly attention to the approach. As Rains has pointed out in her analysis of conceptual divergence within labeling theory, "Social Pathology did not so much set out the framework within which the work of others was then done, but has instead provided a kind of retrospective theoretical touchstone..." (Rains, 1975 p. 2). It should also be noted that Lemert has himself expressed a number of reservations concerning the direction taken by "labeling theory" (cf. Lemert, 1972, pp. 14-24; 1974) indicating that the approach has, in important respects, departed from his earlier formulation of a theory of deviance.

5. Our approach, of necessity, obscures important differences among various theorists within each camp. However, an analysis of those differences would require a separate paper. For an interesting discussion of conceptual divergence within the labeling perspective, see Rains (1975, pp. 1-11). For some of the

points of disagreement within the functionalist perspective, see Cohen (1955, pp. 35-36), Oloward and Ohlin (1960, Ch. 4), and Merton (1968, Ch. 7).

6. Due to space limitations this is a very cursory description of these processes. For further explication, see Parsons (1951, Chap. 6) and Johnson (1960, Chap. 5).

7. It is important to note that the functionalists do not mean by "society" all persons residing within certain geographical boundaries or even in persistent interaction with one another. Rather, "true" membership in a society implies the sharing of an institutional framework, a similar orientation to a pattern of action. See, for example, Levy's (1952, p. 1-127) distinction between "genuine" and "expedient" members of a society.

8. This line of reasoning is not limited to anomie variants of etiological-functionalism. It also characterizes discussions of deviance resulting from role conflict, status disequilibration, etc.

9. Clearly, there is a distinction here between deviance and crime, a distinction which is intrinsic to the functionalist perspective. From this point of view, a criminal act may or may not be deviant. On the other hand, from the labeling perspective, all that is called crime could be subsumed within the category "deviance." For a further discussion of this matter, see Quinney (1965).

10. This conceptualization focuses, of course, on the individual rather than the social system as the point of reference from which deviance is defined. As Parsons notes, "Deviance and the mechanisms of social control may be defined in two ways, according to whether the individual actor or the interactive system is taken as the point of reference. In the first context deviance is a motivated tendency for an actor to behave in contravention of one or more institutionalized normative patterns. . . . In the second context, that of the interactive system, deviance is the tendency on the part of one or more of the component actors to behave in such a way as to disturb the equilibrium of the interactive process..." (Parsons, 1951, p. 250). The variant of the functionalist theory of deviance which is the focus here is predominantly concerned with deviance as defined from the individual point of reference, (e.g., Merton 1938; Cohen, 1955; Cloward and Ohlin, 1960).

11. This crucial feature of the functionalist view of deviance, (i.e., as defined in relation to one who is a "genuine" member of the society whose norms he is violating) is often overlooked or misunderstood. It is not uncommon to see an "unsocialized" or "undersocialized" explanation of deviance attributed to the functionalists (see, for example, Taylor, Walton and Young, 1973, p, 18 and Chambliss, 1975, pp. 8-9). For a discussion of this important (for the functionalists) issue of "membership" in society, see Levy (1952, pp. 122-26).

12. From this perspective, obviously, what is "deviance" is not specified in the world but in the conceptual schema. The root concepts with which functionalists

have been concerned—deviance, conformity, norms, etc.—are "constructed entities," albeit viewed as corresponding to aspects of the external empirical world. The concept "deviance" is not formed in an attempt to mimic the use of similar concepts employed in everyday life (e.g., "criminal," "delinquent," etc.). Rather it is formulated in relation to the other elements of the conceptual scheme of which it is a part. Hence, critics who assert that the functionalist conception of deviance does not incorporate all "real deviance" are missing the entire point of the philosophical stance of analytic realism (see Parsons, 1937, pp. 23-25). Such crass empiricist critiques are well exemplified by Katz's conclusion following his description of several hypothetical cases of witchcraft: "The traditional (functionalist) conception of deviance does not encompass these four cases. Using that conception, we must conclude that these women did not commit deviance, and hence, are not deviants,...But, of course, they are (deviant) as those taking the labelling perspective seem to recognise." (Katz, 1972, p. 188) (emphasis added). Katz seems to assume that what is "truly" deviant is "given in the world" and that the functionalistic conception is "lacking" since it does not incorporate these cases of "truly deviant witchcraft."

13. Gibbs (1966 and 1972) recognizes this important difference between the functionalist and labeling perspectives but fails to relate it systematically to the basis of the conceptual distinction between norms and rules.

14. That is, "deviance" is not conceptually limited to "true" members of a "society" as it is for functionalist analysis (cf. note 4). For further discussion, see Becker's (1963) chapter entitled "Whose Rules?".

15. This is an example of what Becker would call the "falsely accused" (1963, p. 20).

16. This is Becker's (1963, p. 20) "secret deviance" category (a misnomer, to be sure, as the two are a contradiction in terms from his own perspective, notwithstanding his attempt to deal with this in a later discussion, 1973, p. 187). The notion of deviant behavior which is kept secret from others and reacted to only by oneself (i.e., via the norms one has internalized as conscience) makes sense within the functionalists', not the labelists', definition of deviance and the temporal sequence involved.

17. Becker, in his "typology of deviant behavior" implies that rule-violative action does, in cases other than the "falsely accused," indeed precede action. As Katz notes, "By including the 'obedient behavior/rule-breaking behavior' parameter, Becker implies that deviance may be detected by the scientist or independent observer without the aid of the perception and labelling as deviant by community members." (Katz, 1972, p. 189), However, as has been widely noted, (e.g., by Becker himself, 1973, p. 186; and Pollner, 1974, pp. 21-35), this typology is logically inconsistent with Becker's famous conceptualization of deviance (see page 220) as well as with his discussion of rules and reaction

as "problematic." We suggest that Becker's basic position regarding rules, his "typology" aside, is in substantial agreement with what appear to be the positions of symbolic interactionism a la Blumer and ethnomethodology a la Garfinkel. In short, society is an accomplishment; the appearance of rules is something which persons work to create along with the appearance that their behavior conforms to those rules. Or, to put it another way, society is an epiphenomenon. From a labeling standpoint, a rule cannot be said to exist until it is applied (and its application is problematic). There is always a question of the rule's existence. We cannot then suggest that the actor engages in "rule-breaking behavior" unless the rule is applied. Hence, the actor's behavior in occurrence is not "rule-breaking." There is then no rule-breaking behavior—only behavior which is ex post facto subject to being labeled rule-breaking. Similarly, there can, in occurrence, be no "obedient" behavior, only behavior which is not reacted to as "deviant."

18. The distinction between legal and psychological guilt is ours, not Matza's.

19. Another way of conceptualizing "legal guilt" might be in terms of "shame" (in the sense of being shamed, dishonored, disgraced by others).

20. Refer to note 6 for the distinction between this and the functionalists' perspective regarding the relationship (or lack of) between "illegal" and "deviant" behavior.

21. Similar formulations may be found in the writings of Kitsuse (1962, p. 253) and Erickson (1962, p. 308).

22. Traditional symbolic interactionists within the labeling group are not interested in pursuing the etiology of human acts, let alone deviant acts. An "act" is viewed as an idiosyncratic creation of the individual human being. It is associated with the human being's capacity to construct his world independently of causal entities (organic, environmental, or social); hence, the act cannot be explained except in its own terms.

Value Implications of the Functional Theory of Deviance

Charles Wright & R.E. Hilbert

Theories of deviance are often evaluated in terms of their presumably inherent ideological potential. The functional theory of deviance is a case in point. It has been evaluated as inherently conservative, particularly by the "critical criminologists." We argue that such a characterization is superficial and misleading. We examine the theory and conclude that it is not inherently ideological and that indeed its value implications are more radical than is generally thought to be the case.

Much contemporary discussion of theoretical systems in the sociology of deviance and crime focuses about the value-relevance of such systems. Richard Quinney (1977), for example, makes it clear that his dissatisfaction with previously developed systems of criminological theory in large part derives from their socio-political grounding and their ideological implications. However, Quinney's argument is at best superficial and misleading. For example, he argues:

> Rather than exploring alternatives to a capitalist social order, and providing a critique of the existing order, sociologists have tended to furnish ideas that would support the capitalist system (Quinney, 1977: 148).

From Quinney's perspective, certain theories cannot do what a "good theory" should do: Provide an ideological basis for the changes he regards as desirable:

Previously published in *Social Problems* 1980, V. 28 (2): 205-19.

In being ideologically conservative, ahistorical and situational, these sociologies fail to provide the ideas necessary for the transition to socialism (Quinney, 1977: 148).

Quinney and other "critical criminologists" rarely confront alternative theories directly;[1] rather, they simply point out how the theories are ideologically repugnant—given their own goals.

In this paper we examine the theoretical system which has been the favorite target of the "criminal criminologist," the functional theory of deviance. We believe that this theoretical system has yet to be neutralized, even ideologically, by the critique offered in contemporary work, and that the functional theory of deviance does not lend support to capitalism as the "critical criminologists" suggest. Indeed, in our view, it calls attention to problematic aspects of capitalism as a species of modern society with an incisiveness equal to that of "critical criminology." Why, then, is it not regarded as a radical critique of capitalism? We argue, first, that unlike critical criminology the functional theory does not present itself as ideology; second, it proposes no easy or glib solutions to the problems of modern society, including the problems of inequality of opportunity and crime; third, it offers no more support to socialism as an alternative mode of economic organization than it does to capitalism. In sum, it does not provide easy grist for a propaganda mill; that is, it does not furnish a scientific basis either for the values Quinney supports or for the very different values supported by James Q. Wilson (1975).

Value Neutrality

The functionalist's position on value neutrality has two major premises. One is the Kantian distinction between judgments of ultimate value and judgments of fact. According to this view, judgments of ultimate value (those concerning ends) cannot be derived in any sense from experience.[2] That is, one can never know through science whether an act is ultimately right or wrong. What this means is that while statements capable of being tested by reference to facts may have implications for action, they can never directly support that action. On the other hand, it is clear that such statements may be taken as supportive of action, and when they are, they may be referred to as ideological (Parson, 1951; Chpt. 8).

The second basis of the value-neutral position of the functionalist does not raise philosophical problems, but rather political ones concerning the role of the scientist. The prevailing view among functionalists is that the scientist should be oriented exclusively to the development of empirically verifiable cognitive knowledge. There is obviously a value judgment involved in this position, as Parsons recognized explicitly in his early work on the subject:

> It is not an advocacy that the social scientist abstain from value commitments. . . . The point is rather that *in his role* as scientist a particular sub-value system must be paramount for the investigator, that in which conceptual clarity, consistency and generality on the one hand, empirical verifiability on the other are the valued outputs of the process of investigation. . . . Value freedom I thus interpret as the freedom to pursue the values of science within the relevant limits, without their being overridden by values either contradictory to or irrelevant to scientific investigation. . . . At the same time it involves the renunciation of any claims that the scientist qua scientist speaks for value position, on the broader basis of social or cultural significance than that of his science (Parsons, 1971: 33).

In short, the value complex associated with science is seen as paramount in orienting the scientist in the role as scientist. Thus, it is only with respect to issues other than those governing science itself that the scientist *qua* scientist is value neutral.

Values and the Structure of Science

Clearly, then, the value-neutral position adopted by the functionalist does not ignore the role of values in which scientific activity and thought are grounded. Indeed, it would be strange if functionalists, who see values as primary influences upon human conduct, were to ignore the part values play at virtually every stage of the scientific enterprise. For example, there is explicit recognition of their role in the formulation of scientific problems. Commenting on the scientific interest in the actions of human beings, Parsons takes the position that:[3]

> Our interest in them [such actions] is directly determined by their relevance to the values which either the scientist himself shares, or which are significant to him by agreement with his own values or conflict with them. It is this 'relevance to value' (*Wertbeziehung*) which constitutes the selective organizing principle for the empirical material of the social sciences (Parsons, 1937: 573).

Not only is the choice of what to study based upon values, so is the conceptual scheme by which the material is approached. For example, Parsons argues:

> By relevance to such [value] systems the same concrete materials will give rise not to one historical individual but to as many as there are, in this sense, points of view from which to study it. It is, in turn, in the process of analysis of the historical individual and comparison of it with others that general concepts are built up. It follows then that the process will not issue in one ultimately uniform system of general concepts but in as many systems as there are value points of view or others significant to knowledge (Parsons 1937: 593).

It should be noted that this position does not deny the distinction made earlier between fact and value. Nor does it justify the intrusion of value judgments into the analysis of the causes and consequences of an object of study:

> Value judgments (*Wertungen*) cannot claim the objective validity of science, and science must as a methodological ideal, be kept free from them. Even though a value element enters into the selection of the material of science, once this material is given it is possible to come to objectively valid conclusions about the causes and consequences of a given phenomenon free of value judgments. . .(Parsons, 1937: 595).

An important implication of this position is that as scientific study progresses the part played by values steadily recedes and more and more judgments are influenced by questions which the theoretical system itself specifies as relevant.

Clearly, for the functionalist the relationship between fact and value is a subtle one. First, questions of ultimate value cannot be answered by reference to facts. On the other hand, values influence the development of factual knowledge at every stage of the scientific enterprise. Nevertheless, with respect to the role of scientist, it is argued that the scientist *qua* scientist should remain oriented primarily to the subvalue system of science, rather than participate in political disputes.[4]

The Functional Theory of Deviance and Modern Society[5]

The point of view. Functional theorists do not, by and large, advocate solutions to the "problem" of deviance. They locate the source of deviance in the structural features of the system. From this analysis it is possible to infer conservative, moderate, or radical recipes for change, depending upon one's values and the price one is willing to pay. However, the preferred solution does not follow from the terms of the theory itself.

Each substantive theory of functionalism[6] to which we shall refer implicates institutions intrinsic to advanced industrial societies of the American type. Each focuses upon the role of certain institutions in the explanation of deviation from these institutions as well as others within the society. Merton's (1967) theory of anomie is a prime example. In commenting on that theory and arguing that it contains the seeds of a radical critique of American society, Gouldner quite correctly sees that anomie is:

> [T]he unanticipated outcome of social institutions that thwarted men in their effort to acquire the *very* goods and values that these same institutions had encouraged them to pursue. In its openness to the internal contradictions of capitalis*t culture* few Lukacians have been more incisive (Gouldner, 1974; xi).

In our view, each of the functional theorist's (even to some extent Durkheim, 1951, and Parsons, 1951) have pointed to the same type of "internal contradictions" as did Merton. At the basis of all functional theories of deviance is the recognition of the expectation that one pursue the culturally favored goals of the society. It is the *acceptance* of this expectation that generates the deviance. Hence, at the basis of the theory is the internal contradiction—a dialectical relation in that societal institutions provoke their antithesis in the form of departures from, and attacks upon, themselves.

An examination of the substantive theories associated with this perspective will show that the features of the "American Way" of life that are at the root of the problem are among the most cherished features of that way of life. It is not those things which are abhorred by Americans—such as broken homes, alcoholism and negligent parents—which generate deviation, but the structural features of society that are socially prized. Thus functionalists reject the widely held doctrine that "evil is the cause of evil" in human society:

> People are prone to assume that those things which we define as evil and those which we define as good have their origins in separate and distinct features of our society. Evil flows from poisoned wells; good flows from pure and crystal fountains. The same source cannot feed both. Our view is different. It holds *that those values which are at the core of 'the American way of life,'* which help to motivate the behavior *which we esteem as 'typically American,' are among the major determinants of that which we stigmatize as 'pathological'* (Cohen, 1955: 137; emphasis added).

Cohen's contribution to the functional theory is a revision of the theory of anomie. In substance, he argues that the culture of the delinquent gang can be traced to the acceptance by lower-class adolescent males of the middle-class measuring rod, a set of standards which they are not prepared meet.

The indicted institutions. We now turn to a closer examination of the institutional sources of the pressures toward deviance to which the functional theory directs our attention. Our goal is to set the stage for a discussion of the implications for change. Merton, it will be remembered, was concerned first with variations in rates of deviance *between* societies of the American type (in which goal attainment is emphasized rather than the norms prescribing legitimate means to these goals) and societies of the ritualistic type (in which the reverse is the case). The substance of this aspect of his thesis is that one can expect higher rates of deviance in societies of the American type, as compared with societies of the ritualistic type, because the relatively greater emphasis on goal attainment in the former renders the norms prescribing legitimate means ineffective in controlling their illegitimate correlates. *Deviance can thus be traced to an inordinate emphasis on the attainment of certain common success goals.* In Merton's own words "a cardinal American virtue, 'ambition,' promotes a cardinal American vice, 'deviant behavior'" (Merton, 1957: 146). This aspect of Merton's thesis, it should be noted, predicts deviance at all levels within the class structure of societies of the American type, among the rich as well as the poor, the powerful as well as the powerless.

Merton was concerned, second, with differences in rates of deviance *within* societies of the American type. To summarize: Given the tendency toward deviance in societies which emphasize goal attainment more than norms prescribing legitimate means, one can expect the tendency to be even greater among those classes of persons whose access to legitimate means is limited. This aspect of Merton's thesis has been used to explain the higher rates of crime in the lower classes as "revealed" by official statistics on arrest rates; it has become the focus of attention of the majority of sociologists who cite his work on anomie (Hilbert and Wright, 1979); it seems to promise a solution to the problem of anomie within the context of the "American Way," and it is consistent with the liberal values held by many American sociologists. However, the promise may be more apparent than real if, for structural reasons, it is not possible to reduce the level of the inequality of opportunity beyond a certain point. But more of this later.

The liberal solution to the problem posed by Merton's analysis is to equalize opportunity and to institutionalize it in some form of meritocracy, as Merton himself proposed. Taylor comments:

> Merton in his later more policy oriented work would solve the problem of anomie by two strategies: first, success must be based upon merit and second (in order to implement this) there must be ample opportu-

nities. . . .The central dictum should be 'from those according to their merit, to each according to his merit. . .' (Taylor et al., 1974: 104).

Whether or not Merton believed that a complete meritocracy can be structured within an industrial society, much less a capitalistic one, is unclear. What does seem clear is that a higher level of institutionalization of achievement criteria would not decrease the problem to which Cohen (1955) refers; rather it would increase it. For Cohen the disabilities faced by the working-class child are the result of a pattern of socialization, the form and content of which is dictated by working-class values. If, as Cohen suggests, these values are adaptive for persons in the lower reaches of the class structure, then they are likely to remain with us as long as there is inequality in the distribution of rewards. The implications of Cohen's position seems clear: Meritocracy will, if anything, aggravate the problem faced by the lower-class child. We will return to this implication later.

The liberal reform solution to the problem that Cohen presents usually involves the advocacy of more efficient ways of imparting "protestant-bourgeois" culture to the lower classes. The suggested mode of inculcation usually involves ameliorative programs such as "Head Start" or state proposals designed to intervene in the transmission and/or break up of the "culture of poverty." One result of such programs, as Cloward and Ohlin (1960: Chpt. 8) point out, has been the destruction of the "integrated" slum and a weakening of the illegitimate opportunity structures" historically found therein. These structures, it will be recalled, provide investment capital, political power, and thus the basis for the development of legitimate opportunity. Ironically, the net effect of ameliorative welfare state programs has been to reduce opportunity by destroying structures which have served as mechanisms of escape from such communities.

For Merton, then, the origin of the pressure toward deviance is to be found first and foremost in the "overweening" emphasis upon success goals instituted throughout the class structure of society. If a more endemic and characteristic feature of American social organization can be imagined, then it must be Cohen's emphasis which finds the source of deviance in the American (and, more generally, Occidental) "industrial achievement motif." In short, Merton and Cohen focus upon two *related* and essential features of the American way of life as the primary sources of deviance: (1) the widely diffused acquisitive impulse and (2) the "bureaucratic ethos." Both of these have been associated with capitalism and industry in the work of Weber (1958). Cohen recognizes this in his discussion of the "Middle Class Ethos" as the locus of the problem: "[T]hese norms are, in effect, a tempered version of the Protestant Ethic which has played such an important part in the shaping of the American character and American society" (Cohen, 1955: 87). Again, it is to the central features of modern industrial societies to which these theories point as a major source of deviance. If one seeks to solve the problem by going to its source, it is clear that these societies must be fundamentally reordered. Above all, there is no suggestion in functional theory that "tinkering around" with society is going to solve the problems toward which the theory directs our attention, as its liberal defenders and its radical critics tend to believe. Its implications are either more radical or, given a certain pessimism, more conservative than the advocates of "tinkering" realize.

The "solutions" to the problem of deviance implied by functional analysis will be examined more thoroughly in the next section as we consider the question of why functional theory is so often seen as conservative.

Functional Theory's Conservative Pessimism

In explaining the emergence of deviance, functional theory focuses upon social structure and implicates those institutions which are basic to industrial society. Given the assumption that high rates of deviance are undesirable, one might expect the analysis of the functionalist to be regarded as radical. However, it has not been. More often than not is has been taken to be a conservative doctrine, a defense rather than a critique of the existing institutional system. There are several reasons why.

The inevitability of crime and the function of punishment. First, modern functionalism accepts Durkheim's conclusion that crime in human society is normal or inevitable. As Durkheim put it, "in the first place crime is normal because a society exempt from it is utterly impossible" (Durkheim, 1964: 64). Durkheim's argument is that society is a moral order, which means its boundaries are defined by moral norms. Tendencies toward deviance can be controlled only by the most successful kind of socialization in which the norms are implanted uniformly in all individuals and deeply enough to deter the expression of all desires to the contrary. He believed that the process of socialization is not likely ever to be that successful and even if it were crime would not thereby disappear—for in strengthening the common consciousness, acts would be defined as crime which were before "simple moral faults." The "problem" here is the result of the fact that the moral norms not only control behavior they define it as well.

This position has been maintained in functionalism through the work of Parsons (1951) and Kai Erickson (1966). In addition, functionalists find persuasive Durkheim's argument that punishment is functionally necessary in *any* moral order, regardless of its substance (see Durkheim, 1964; Erickson, 1966; and Parsons, 1951). These suggestions militate against the development of the optimism which undergirds much advocacy of social change. On the other hand, they do not preclude the advocacy of change as a solution to the problems of crime and deviance. Rather, they tend to establish "conditional limits" within which proposals for change must be developed if they are to be regarded as realistic. There is nothing in functional theory which implies that all societies give rise to the same amount or types of crime and deviation, or that structural change might not eliminate some of the sources of acts so defined. As a result, these features of functional theory are among the least salient of those which explain why functionalism is understood as a conservative doctrine. Certainly they are not as often alluded to by the radical critics of functionalism as are other features of the theoretical system. More important in the critique of functionalism in this regard are two features of its analytic apparatus: 1) the consensual paradigm and 2) its systemic character.

The consensual starting point. Functionalism starts with consensus and ask, "How do diversity, innovation, or deviance emerge?" From the very beginning, it focuses on those features of social life where there is consensus and hence reciprocity and coordination—features over which there is no fundamental disagreement. But consensual agreement is not to be taken as descriptive of any specific social system; functionalists understand well that there has never been a social system in which there is total agreement on anything. Consensus is simply a point of departure for the analysis of social order, including disorder.[7] In their concern with the "problem of order," functionalists have asked how order emerges out of conflict, how threats to order are overcome and even how disconsensus (e.g., through adaptive structures) contributes to order. Conflict is being dealt with constantly by functionalists. Nevertheless, because of the consensual starting point, certain politically relevant problems (e.g., of war, of disarticulated slave-master relationships and, more generally, of superordination and subordination in which power rather than authority are involved) tend to be underplayed or ignored altogether.

As one might expect, deviance and crime are conceived as taking place within an established consensus. The possibility that crime is a function of law emerging out of conflict between persons in fundamental disagreement with one another is precluded by the perspective. Explanations for crime which view it as a function of oppression or as an effort to colonize a segment of a population are also precluded because they take one outside the conceptual frame of the perspective, beyond its most fundamental assumptions about the nature of social life. Such explanations (perhaps focusing upon the clash between opposing consensual groups) would take us into the arena of fundamental disconsensus, to relations between aliens, to conflict outside the framework of institutional life, to power rather than authority, to basic disagreements of interest and value. Put another way, radical conflict is outside the perspective, an "intersocietal" rather than an "intrasocietal" phenomenon.[8] Since it is out of concern for segmentation, radical conflict, struggles for power, and oppression that radicalism frequently emerges, it is not surprising that functionalism rarely comes off radical—except in spite of itself.

The systemic organization of theory. A third factor, one of primary importance in the assessment of functionalism's conservative character, is its systemic, "holistic" character. The assumption of systemic functional analysis is a relationship between social and cultural items such that they influence one another in fundamental ways. When relations are systemic, any change in one component will have consequences for the rest of the system; that is, a change in one social item sets up pressure for adjustment and more fundamental change in the remaining units of the system. Hence any alterations in society may have far-reaching consequences. Such a "realization" may, in itself, lead to some caution in the advocacy of social change.

Before continuing with various proposed solutions to the problems posed by functional theory, it is essential to consider what functionalists are saying about the positive functional significance of common success goals. These goals are so important that they can be eliminated only at great cost to the society, according to the theory. As Cloward and Ohlin posed the issue succinctly some years ago:

> A crucial problem in the industrial world . . . is to locate and train the most talented persons in every generation, irrespective of the vicissitudes of birth to occupy technical work roles. Whether he is born into wealth or poverty, each individual, depending upon his ability and diligence must be encouraged to find his 'natural level' in the social order. This problem is one of tremendous proportions. Since we cannot know in advance who can best fulfill the requirements of various occupational roles, *the matter is presumably settled through the process of competition.* But how can men throughout the social order be motivated to participate in this competition. . . . It is not enough for a few to make the race: *all must be motivated to strive, so that the most able and talented will be the victors in the competitive struggle for higher status.*

> One of the ways in which industrial society attempts to solve this problem is by *defining success-goals as potentially accessible to all,* regardless of race, creed, or socioeconomic position. Great social rewards, it is said, are available to anyone, however lowly his origins. ... The industrial society, in short, emphasizes *common* or universal success-goals as a way of assuring its survival (Cloward and Ohlin, 1960: 82; emphasis added).[9]

A crucial function is then performed in industrial society by the diffusion of "lofty goals" throughout the class structure: The talented, as well as the not so talented, are motivated to perform by the promise of wealth, status and power. This must be done so the process of personal recruitment can proceed. Hence, persons are motivated to perform and to get into the race regardless of their class origins. In order to instill the necessary motivational level, it is essential that people believe that they have a realistic opportunity to succeed. That is, at least the appearance of equality of opportunity must exist, even in the lower reaches of society. Hence combined with this diffusion of goals we find a "democratic ethos" which dictates that because all have an equal chance to succeed, all are obliged to try. But, as the theory of deviance also emphasizes, we do not all have an equal chance to succeed. Some are frustrated in the pursuit of goals they are induced to want and encouraged to seek. Deviance emerges as a possible solution to this frustration.

Implications for Action

Given the crucial functions of the diffusion of goals and of democratic ideology within industrial society, what can be done to alleviate the problem of deviance?

The Liberal Solution

The liberal solution, consistent with American ideology, is to equalize opportunity. As has been indicated, this solution involves the establishment of meritocracy and is not viable within the framework of the theory itself. Meritocracy is impossible given two outstanding conditions which functionalism finds inevitable in human societies. The first is inequality in the structure of rewards, the second, affectivity and diffuse role obligations in the family. We are well aware that meritocracy does not imply the establishment of "equality," only "equality of opportunity" to perform and hence be rewarded. But such equality of opportunity is not possible as long as inequalities of wealth and power persist alongside the existence of the family or something structurally similar. Meritocracy demands that universalistic achievement criteria be the sole basis of evaluation operating in the distribution of rewards in society. In the family and related institutions evaluation is particularistic and ascriptive. Further, because of the character and necessity of socialization of the young, something like the family as we know it must exit. That is, a structure characterized by affectivity and diffuse role obligations must operate in society in order to accomplish the functionally relevant tasks of the historic family. Second, institutions similarly characterized and much valued (such as friendship) carry on (as does the family) not only socialization functions but tension management functions as well. Such institutional relations, although perhaps hard to come by in a budding meritocracy, will fill a crucial need for the management of anxiety generated by naked competition (see Young, 1961). In short, functionally inevitable inequalities of power and wealth, combined with the persistence of functionally necessary remnants of community (such as family), will prevent the establishment of meritocracy and true "equality of opportunity." As long as some fathers have more power than other fathers, they will see to it that their children get "breaks" which they do not feel obliged to provide for other children; that is, particularistic advantage will accrue to the offspring of the powerful. Lenksi illustrated quite a while ago how this tendency operates in the Soviet Union:

> This relative lack of job security, however, has not prevented the Soviet managerial class from becoming semihereditary. Judging from available evidence, it appears that managers who remain in the good graces of the party elite can secure for their children special educational advantages which, as elsewhere, pave the road to membership in

the managerial class or one of the other privileged segments of Soviet society. Khrushchev himself stated that only a third of the students at the university level were the children of peasants in the 1950's. A recently expatriated Soviet student reports that 'only a handful of students attending the prestige institutions come from families outside the intelligentsia, and that the greater the prestige of the university or institute, the more elite are those who attend it.' Since the managerial class is counted among the rukovadiaschie Kadry, or leading cadres, within the intelligentsia it is safe to assume that its sons are well represented in the best universities and institutes (Lenski, 1966: 357).

It would appear, then, that even in the Soviet Union where the advantages associated with inherited wealth have been reduced, the children of the successful have advantages over the children of the unsuccessful.[10] The conclusion seems obvious: Given the orientation of the family toward affectivity, particularism, and diffuse role obligations, inequality of opportunity is likely to "rear its ugly head" even where there are deliberate efforts to keep it under control.

It should also be pointed out that even if meritocracy could be instituted, it would be no solution to the problem to which Cohen (1955) directs our attention; in fact, it is itself the problem. A strict meritocratic regime would simply enhance the bind in which the lower- and working-class children are placed: Their situation would be made more difficult as long as they were not equipped by early socialization to live within such a regime. Again the issue is implied by the functional theory of stratification. As long as there are inequalities of power and wealth (which this theory finds inevitable in industrial societies) one may expect a "culture of deprivation" to emerge and, one institutionalized, to function as an adjustive mechanism which "cools out" and thus "ameliorates" the condition of those who are denied. There is no reason to believe that those who are socialized within this milieu and culture will be equipped to perform by the standards of ascetic Protestantism of the dominate class. Deferred gratification makes no sense in a lower-class world presenting limited opportunity for upward mobility. From a number of vantage points within functional theory, liberal solutions to the problem of deviance appear as a pipedream.[11]

The Socialist Solution

The socialist solution includes the establishment of a system of social rewards based on the proposition, "from each according to his ability, to each according to his needs." This, of course, is to be accomplished through the abolition of privately-owned productive property. Within the Marxian framework such property lies at the basis of power differentials, authority relations, and the existence of alienation. Within the terms of functional theory the feasibility of such a solution fails on some of the same obstacles as the liberal solution, although for different reasons. One of the problems faced by the advocates of socialism is how to overcome the tendencies toward inequality in the distribution of rewards for work within the context of industrial society (see Freeman, 1979; cf. Lenski, 1978). Often there is a correlative concern with overcoming tendencies toward competition and the pursuit of self-interest, both of which are empirically related to inequality. The implication of the functional theory (of stratification) is that you cannot overcome either set of tendencies. Inequality is (functionally) necessary for motivating the high levels of performance required by such societies, especially in connection with the more technical work roles. It is conceded by functionalists that one might attain a measure of equality within a "community of believers." However, this would not be possible in the long run presumably, and especially if there are large numbers of technical work roles to be filled and carried out efficiently. The persistence of inequality in the Soviet Union, and the recent shift toward inequality in the reward structure of China, would be interpreted by the functionalists as necessary because of the emphasis on performance in both societies. Given the historical failure of attempts to institutionalize equality within industrial societies, the burden of proof is on those persons who would agree that it is possible.

There is another equally fundamental objection within functional theory to the socialist solution. Operating within the legacy of Max Weber, rather than Karl Marx, functionalists do not find the existence of private productive property at the root of alienation in modern societies. The definitive quality of capitalism is not found to be private property, but the "rational calculation of cost and gain" and, more generally, the "rational cast of mind." Socialism, rather than being viewed as a major transformation of capitalism, is its logical extension.[12] Socialism is but an enhanced version of capitalism's basic motif—bureaucratic planning, centralization and rationality. Insofar as socialism is so regarded, the issue is again shifted to the problem to which Cohen directs us. That is, if socialism cannot meet its ideal—humanistic allocation of rewards in terms of humanistic consideration—but rather is meritocratic as Weber would have it, then like liberalism it simply exacerbates the problem of children ill-equipped to meet the performance demands of a bureaucratic social order.[13]

The Conservative Solution

The third solution to the problem, which may be referred to as conservative, is to reestablish "castelike" relations between the various strata of the population. The object here is to reduce mobility aspirations. Reducing the aspirations of those not realistically in a position to succeed will have the effect of reducing frustration. In this case the elimination of the "malintegrated" social structure to which Merton and Cloward and Ohlin refer is not to be realized by the equalization of opportunity but the "stratification of aspirations."

This solution is at least as vulnerable as those dealt with earlier. By reducing commitments to common success goals, lower-class persons would be less motivated to perform, to do those things that one must do in order to succeed. One would expect persons in the higher classes also to be less motivated to perform, as the number of lower-class persons in competition for these goals is reduced. In addition, any significant reduction in commitment to common success goals can be expected to decrease the rate of upward mobility and the rate at which talent will be developed and utilized. The result would be a tendency to fill positions in terms of qualities rather than performance criteria, which is certain to have a depressing effect on productivity. There is no good reason to believe that the son of a physicist, by virtue of that fact, will be able or willing to "fill his father's shoes."[14] Finally, there would be a tendency to return to the kind of "traditionalism" in the workplace which Weber described as characteristic of the period prior to the Reformation. The cost in terms of productivity seems obvious (see Cloward and Ohlin, 1960: Chpt. 4).

Functionalism's Value Implications

It appears, then, that it is not correct to say that functionalism is an inherently conservative doctrine. Neither the conservative nor the liberal solution is any more viable than the socialist solution. All of these solutions fail to solve the problem, exacerbate it, or fail to provide a basis for meeting the minimum conditions for the existence of industrial society. Further, it is not accurate to suggest that the functional theory of deviance presents a defense of the status quo. It actually identifies the existing institutional framework as the source of the problem. Nevertheless, it may be true that many proponents of functional theory tend to accept the basic features of American society (see Gouldner, 1970). If this is the case, the reasons should now be clear: The proposed alternatives appear, on balance, to be no more likely than the "American Way" to provide solutions to the dilemmas posed by their theory. One is reminded at this point of Gouldner's description of objectivity in the social sciences:

> Objectivity is the way one comes to terms and makes peace with a world one does not like but will not oppose; it arises when one is detached from the status quo but reluctant to be identified with its critics, detached from the dominant map of social reality as well as from the meaningful alternative maps (Gouldner, 1970: 103).

It just may be that part of the motivation for the posture we call objectivity, in the case of the functionalist at any rate, is the pessimism which their theories generate.

The designation of the functional theory of deviance as both pessimistic and conservative also should be clear. It is as critical of capitalist society as is critical criminology, but its conclusion, that none of the proposed alternatives is likely to solve the problems posed by the theory, provides no substantial basis for being optimistic about the success of any efforts at change. Its description of industrial society as "Hell" is not the thing that disturbs us, but the fact that it provides "no exit" (see Gouldner, 1955).

Before concluding, it seems appropriate to comment on perhaps the most pointed solution to come from the socialists: The decentralization of socialist organization. At least some of these solutions appear to question the value of industrial life and "rationality" as they look toward the establishment of a modified version of community. We may assume that, as a result, individualistic competition and meritocratic evaluation would at least be tempered and that there would be a certain cost with respect to productive and administrative efficiency. Furthermore, "community" may involve the loss of modern consciousness, of cosmopolitanism, relativism, and the dereification of institutions associated with modern society. Quinney's suggestion as to what form the "new order" should take, while attractive in terms of its emphasis on democracy and local control, is also frightening in its emphasis on regulation of behavior through the internalization of moral norms:

> A contemporary experience that gives support to the possibility of community custom is the case of revolutionary Cuba. . . . Neighborhoods in Cuba now have their own courts, staffed by personnel elected democratically from in the community. Little emphasis is placed on sanctions of any kind. Instead, violators continue to be educated within the community. Custom plays as educative role within the community rather than a punitive one. What is important is maintain peace in the community rather than enforcement of a legal system (Quinney, 1973: 191).

Quinney's commitment to order is evident. His "critique of legal order" is that it is not order at all, but "disorder." More importantly, he either does not realize the sacrifices in "freedom" which order entails or does not mind making them. "Education" rather than punishment suggests, if not the "therapeutic state," then the not so self-conscious but more efficient "upright and uptight" community of conformity, "order" and dulled consciousness. The cost of community may be too great. It may not only be technique, industrial development, and achievement which will be sacrificed, but also individual integrity and freedom. High rates of deviation mean disorder, but disorder may be the cost of political freedom and a liberated consciousness. Quinney is right—legal disorder is a substitute for moral order. What is puzzling is his preference.

Quinney's view of the nature of the "new community"[15] suffers from more problems than we are prepared to go into at this time. We would like to suggest, however, that a moral community that is "nonpunitive" in response to violation is not a moral community at all (see Durkheim, 1938).

Some Final Remarks

Clearly, the aim of this paper has not been to expunge value questions from the discourse of deviance. Quite the contrary, we have sought to focus attention upon such questions—but not unadvisedly. We seek to avoid confounding ideology and science and smuggling values into discourse under the rubric of science. Further, we do not accept the elaborate (yet unconvincing) arguments emanating from the school of "Critical Theory" that the distinction between cognitive and evaluative questions or orientations is spurious. We take the position that morals are neither revealed nor the product of scientific investigation, but rather a *priori* human constructions. This seems to be the point Mills was making when he argued. "I have never found either a transcendent or an imminent ground for moral judgment. The only moral values I hold I got from right inside history" (Domhoff and Ballard, 1970: 246).

Our objective has been to contribute to the analysis of the strains associated with advanced industrial societies, by bringing together some of the fundamental insights of functional analysis and assessing their implications for certain values. What we offer should be useful to those who are interested in altering or transforming the systems under consideration. Indeed, insofar as the analysis is correct, to ignore it might be quite costly. If this paper contains any message for contemporary advocates of social change (including Marxists and Critical Theorists), it is that the "limiting conditions" toward which functional analysis directs our attention should be carefully considered. If one's theoretical alternatives are limited, so too is one's praxis. Functionalism has, in a sense, brought some bad news; but rather than slay the messenger one ought to carefully scrutinize the message.

With respect to the range of proposed solutions to the problem of advanced industrial societies, in particular the high rates of deviance, each of the suggestions reviewed here involves some "costs." Because they appear naïve, some proposals would seem impracticable. This is particularly true of the "liberal solutions." Others—the conservative and those we've classified as socialistic—involve "losses," either in human freedom or in the economic production, or both. However, it is easy to imagine that many would willingly "suffer" such losses if they were assured an increase in the level of equality in the distribution of goods and services and in the level of equality of opportunity. Proposals of this sort may become more acceptable as we come to recognize that resource depletion and environmental degradation are inevitable outcomes of the emphasis on productivity and industrial-technical development. Such proposals, whether capitalist or socialist, would very likely have as their objective, a "powering down" of the economy. More important, they would result in the attenuation of the emphasis upon "overarching (material) success goals" characteristic of modern societies, as well as upon "meritocratic achievement." Finally, change in this direction should result in a lower level of occupational specialization, occupational stratification, and status differentiation associated with occupation and income.

No doubt there are problems associated with such changes which we do not now foresee; but change in this direction might well reduce the stresses and strains intrinsic to modern society toward which functional theorists have directed our attention in their explanation of the high rates of deviance in such societies. Also, the "powering down" of the economies of modern societies, combined with some form or the other of socialistic organization, could conceivably result in greater equality in the distribution of wealth, as well as equality of opportunity, but only at the cost of efficiency and production incentives. The "cost" in connection with such a move may be tolerable if it is not so severe as to involve a generalized decline in the vitality of the population. With respect to socialism and production incentives, Peter Berger remarks:

> The intrinsically allocative orientation of socialism almost certainly inhibits individual efforts to achieve. Where the allocative principle has been realized most fully (as in the Chinese and Cuban policies of "moral incentives"), the decline in productivity appears to have been sharp (in both cases forcing a revision of the policy). The aforementioned data on agricultural productivity strongly suggest that peasants work better for private than for public gain. Thus it has been argued that, if capitalism has introduced a dynamic principle of rationality into economic production, socialism has a built in tendency to revert to the awkward and inefficient habits associated with premodern social systems (Berger, 1976: 86).

We are inclined to think that such changes would never be acceptable within America (where the dominant sectors of the population are committed to "production," "achievement" and "growth," conceived as "progress") if it were not for the threat of fossil fuel depletion, the difficulty of developing functional alternatives to this source of energy, and the recognition of environmental problems. A careful weighing of the evidence would suggest that most Americans are willing to tolerate high rates of deviance rather than make fundamental changes in their way of life. It remains to be seen whether they can live with the very serious problems associated with resource depletion and environmental degradation. It is not surprising that suggestions that Americans may have to learn to live with less have emanated even from the White House and from former presidential candidate, Governor Jerry Brown.

In conclusion, we agree with Max Weber that it is unlikely

that the grip of the remnants of ascetic Protestantism, as manifest in what he called the "mechanized petrification" of contemporary social life, will be easily loosened:

> This order is now bound to the technical and economic conditions of machine production which today determines the lives of all the individuals who are born into this mechanism, not only those concerned with economic acquisition, with irresistible force. Perhaps it will so determine them until the last ton of fossilized coal is burnt (Weber, 1958: 181).

At the same time the prospect of the burning of this last ton (or barrel) may act as a lever by which the "powering down" of these economies will be accomplished, and in such a way as to attenuate not only the problem of energy resource depletion and environmental destruction, but the problem of deviance to which the functionalists have called our attention.

References

Berger, Peter
    1976 *Pyramids of Sacrifice,* Garden City, N.J.: Anchor Press.

Cohen, Albert
    1955 *Delinquent Boys,* New York: Free Press.

Cloward, R. and L. Ohlin
    1960 *Delinquency and Opportunity,* New York: Free Press.

Davis, Kinglsey and Wilbert Moore
    1945 "Some principles of stratification." *American Sociologist Review* 10: 242-247.

Domhoff, G. and H. Ballard
    1970 *C. Wright Mills and the Power Elite,* Boston: Bacon.

Durkheim, Emile
    1951 *Suicide.* New York: Free Press. [1897]
    1964 *The Rules of Sociological Method.* New York: Free Press. [1894]

Erikson, Kai
    1966 *Wayward Puritans: A Study in the Sociology of Deviance.* New York: Wiley.

Freeman, Harold
    1979 "Toward socialism in America." *Monthly Review* 31, 4: 21-29

Gouldner, A.

1955 "Metaphysical pathos and the theory of bureaucracy," *American Political Science Review* 49: 496-508.

1970 *The Coming Crisis of Western Sociology.* New York: Basic Books.

1974 "Preface." In I. Taylor et al., *The New Criminology.* New York: Harper and Row.

Hilbert, R. E. and Charles Wright

1979 "Representations of Merton's theory of anomie." *The American Sociologist* 14:150-56.

Lenski, Gerhard

1966 *Power and Privilege.* New York: McGraw-Hill

1978 "Marxist experiments in destratification: An Appraisal." *Social Forces* 57, 2 (Dec.): 364-83.

Matthews, M.

1978 *Privilege in the Soviet Union.* London: George and Unwin.

Marcuse, Herbert

1964 *One-Dimensional Man.* Boston: Beacon.

Merton, Robert

1967 "Social structure and anomie." Pp. 131-60 in *Social Theory and Social Structure.* New York: Free Press.

Parsons, Talcott

1937 *The Structure of Social Action.* New York: McGraw-Hill.

1951 *The Social System.* New York: Free Press.

1954 "An analytical approach to the theory of social stratification." Pp. 69-88 in Essays in [1940] *Sociological Theory.* New York: Free Press.

1954 "A revised analytical approach to the theory of social stratifications." Pp. 386-439 in Essays in [1953] *Sociological Theory.* New York: Free Press.

1954 "Social classes and class conflict in the light of recent sociological theory." Pp. 323-35 in *Essays in Sociological Theory.* New York: Free Press.

1971 "Value freedom and objectivity," Pp.27-50 in Otto Strammer (ed.), *Max Weber and Sociology Today.* New York: Harper and Row.

Piven, Francis Fox and Richard A. Cloward

1971 Regulating the Poor: *The Functions of Public Welfare.* New York: Pantheon Books.

1977 *Poor People's Movements: Why They Succeed, How They Fail.* New York: Pantheon Books.

Quinney, R.

1970 *The Social Reality of Crime.* Boston: Little, Brown.

1973 *Critique of Legal Order.* Boston: Little, Brown.

1977 *Class, State and Crime.* New York: David McKay.

Schaff, Adam
    1970 *Marxism and the Human Individual.* New York: McGraw-Hill.

Taylor, I., P. Walton and J. Young
    1974 *The New Criminology.* New York: Harper and Row.

Weber, Max
    1958 *The Protestant Ethic and the Spirit of Capitalism.* New York: Scribner's.

    1978 *Economy and Society.* G. Roth and Claus Wittich (eds.). Berkeley: University of California Press.

Wilson, J. M.
    1975 *Thinking about Crime.* New York: Basic Books.

Yinger, J. M.
    1970 *The Scientific Study of Religion.* London: Macmillian.

Young, M.
    1961 *The Rise of the Meritocracy.* Baltimore, Marland: Penguin Books.

Endnotes

1. An exception is Taylor et al. (1974); however, in our view, this work does not adequately apprehend the basic framework of a number of the theories which it treats. This is particularly true for functional theory, and characterizes the treatment of Durkheim as well as the more modern functionalist–Merton, Cohen, and Cloward and Ohlin.

2. We do not wish to leave the impression that the position of functionalism suggests that facts have no implications for value judgments. Rather, given an initial premise in the form of a statement of value (e.g., anything which contributes to the attainment of the end-state X is good), a statement of fact concerning the means-end relationship (e.g., Y contributes to the attainment of the end X) may serve as a minor premise, and a contingent value judgment may follow as the logical conclusion (Y is good).

3. This remark is a summary of Weber's position with which Parsons is in substantial agreement. His major reservation is with Weber's limiting these insights to the social sciences. Parsons finds the description equality applicable to the natural sciences.

4. Functionalists (e.g., Parsons) also recognize that scientists' values may distort their perception of the facts, i.e., that some cognitive beliefs are "meaningful" to the observer—that he or she has a "stake in the matter" (Parsons, 1951:Chpt. 8). Such observation is "ideological" in Parsons' terms. However, functionalists are inclined to see this as a methodological problem, mandating that the observer resist this biased perception, rather than as a basis for abandoning the quest for more neutral observation.

5. Some may question the appropriateness of the label "functional theory of deviance" when discussing the *emergence* of deviance rather than its functional significance. We think it is appropriate in at least two respects. First, the theory has been developed by functionalists, utilizing all of the assumptions about the systemic nature of social life characteristic of functional analysis. Second, functionalists regard their analysis as less than complete if they make no attempt to explain the emergence of the phenomena with which they deal functionally. Yinger (1970:93) said that "functional investigation is the study of *the degree to which a* product of the system serves to maintain it, full attention being paid to the balance of support and costs." So part of functional analysis is the explanation of those products of the system which are being assessed functionally; at the same time, some functionalists have considered a wide range of questions, and not all such questions are easily designatable as "questions of functional analysis." The two leading "functionalists," Parsons and Merton, each preferred other designations of their approach: Parsons, "The Theory of Acton"; Merton, "Structuralism."

6. We refer here to three works in particular: 1) Merton's *Social Structure and Anomie* (1938); 2) Cohen's *Delinquent Boys* (1955); and 3) Cloward and Ohlin's *Delinquency and Opportunity* (1960).

7. Although functionalism emphasizes consensus (see Parsons' fundamental paradigm to social interaction, 1951:204-05, and 251-52), this does not imply that empirical societies (as opposed to scientists analytical schemes) are understood as without conflict. With reference to the concept of "adaptive structures," Parsons notes:

> Integration . . . . is a compromise between the functional imperatives in a situation and the dominant value orientation pattern of a society. *Every society is of necessity shot through with such compromise* (Parsons and Shils, 1952:177; emphasis added).

It should be noted that such "compromises" involve conflict at the level of value and interest. Further, Parsons (1954) discusses a number of ways in which societies may generate class conflict.

8. This does not imply that functionalism cannot explain the emergence of radical conflict within a society, only that radical and disconsensus are not its point of departure.

9. The quotation, partly an elaboration of Durkheim and Merton, continues:

> One of the paradoxes of social life is that the processes by which societies seek to ensure order sometimes result in disorder. If a cultural emphasis on unlimited success-goals tends to solve some problems in the industrial society, it also creates new ones. A pervasive feeling of position discontent leads men to compete for higher status and so contributes to the survival of the industrial order, but it also produces acute pressure for deviant

behavior. Unlimited aspirations, Durkheim pointed out, exert an intense pressure toward disorder because they are, by definition, unachievable and thus constitute a source of "uninterrupted agitation."

In more recent work, with Piven, Cloward has concentrated more on "pressure toward disorder," especially by the poor (See Piven and Cloward, 1977, 1977) Their work indicates that scholars using concepts and insights from functional analysis are not necessarily ideological conservatives. (cf. the exchanges with Roach and Roach, *Social Problems* 1978: Vol. 26, Nos. 2 and 3.)

10. Later evidence indicates that this tendency has, if anything, increased its hold in the Soviet Union. For a consideration of the extent of "class privilege" in the Soviet Union, see Matthews (1978, especially part three and the Postscript).

11. The fact that the architects of these theories are more often than not sociopolitical liberals seems not to have prevented them from building theories which do not necessarily articulate with their sociopolitical commitments. This is a possibility that even the most sophisticated students of the sociology of sociology (e.g., Gouldner, 1970) do not properly develop. Objectively yields, of necessity, not "coolness" but a type of passion exemplified by a scholar such as Weber. The necessity is an outcome of the stripping away of layers of sentiment from the self to get at the biases presumed to undermine comprehension. Such a process inevitably "hurts" but is well within the range of expected human behavior. After all, if human beings are capable of self-immolation, perhaps we may expect to discover a few intellectual masochists from time to time.

12. Weber remarks:
> The primary source of the superiority of bureaucratic administration lies in the role of technical knowledge which, through the development of modern technology and business methods of the production of goods, has become completely indispensable. In this respect, it makes no difference whether the economic system is organized on a capitalistic or socialist basis. Indeed, if in the latter case a comparable level of technical efficiency were to be achieved, it would mean a tremendous increase in the importance of professional bureaucrats (Weber, 1978:223-225).

13. A number of prominent modern Marxists have capitulated to Weber's thesis, most notably, Adam Schaff (1970). Even Critical Theory (e.g., Marcuse, 1964) may be seen as substantively consistent with Weber's analysis and prophecy concerning modern society.

14. Functional theory is as much concerned with motivation as it is with talent. Workers at all levels must be willing as well as able to perform their occupational work roles. Then, if industrial societies develop technologies requiring very little skill, demands for a motivated work force would require commitment to common success goals and competition in performance criteria.

15. This "quest for community" is characteristic of many variants of modern Marxism. Just what the "costs" of community are, and how they might avoided in the "new community" is rarely discussed in Marxist literature.

Durkheim and Quinney on The Inevitability of Crime: A Comparative Theoretical Analysis

R. E. Hilbert & Charles W. Wright

This paper compares sociological theories of crime in an effort to expose the function of conceptualization in the process of doing science. In the famous chapter from The Rules of Sociological Method *(1964) on "The Normal and the Pathological," Durkheim suggests that the condition that generates crime is inevitable ("normal") and desirable. Quinney, in his* Critique of Legal Order *(1973), calls on us to imagine a society free of crime. The aim of the paper is to understand these conclusions concerning the inevitability of crime by reference to the distinctive features of the conceptual schemes that were employed in their derivation. Major aspects of the schemes considered are the positions taken concerning the nature of law, the conditions under which law emerges, and the position of the criminal vis-à-vis the group whose sentiments are offended. These aspects are examined in an attempt to present the logical coherence of the two theories as well as the central points of divergence between them.*

The focus of the following paper is on certain conclusions in the work of Emile Durkheim and Richard Quinney concerning the question of the inevitability of crime in modern societies. In his now famous chapter in *The Rules of Sociological Method* (1964a) entitled "The Normal and the Pathological," Durkheim develops the position that crime is inevitable in human societies.[1] In his *Critique of Legal Order* (1974), Quinney takes the position that crime as a legal category of action can be largely, if not completely, eliminated from society. The aims of this paper are, first, to explicate the theories of both men in order to show the way in which they arrived at their respective positions on the question at issue and, second, to comment on the implications of their views for the question of social change as a solution to the "problem" of crime.

Given the first of these aims, the paper may obviously be seen as an analysis of the substance of the views of Durkheim and Quinney on a question of considerable importance to the sociologist interested in the study of crime. But it may be seen as more than this. It is also an exercise is comparative theory. With respect to the latter, it is our view that an understanding of conflicting substantive conclusions can be enhanced by an analysis of the primary concepts in terms of which the positions are developed. Among other things, such an analysis is likely to reveal the critical aspects of the conceptualization, those which are heavily implicated in the formation of substantive conclusions. With respect to the importance that we attach to this matter, we acknowledge the influence of Parsons (1937):

> It is fundamental that there is no empirical knowledge which is not in some sense and to some degree conceptually formed. All talk of "pure sense data," "raw experience" of the unformed stream of consciousness is not descriptive of actual experience (p. 28).

It is then to the conceptual scheme that we turn, with special interest in the way it "forms" the phenomena to which it directs attention.

Moreover, with respect to the questions raised by the sociology of knowledge, comparative analysis may contribute to our understanding of the acceptance of a given theoretical position,

---

1. He also argues that crime is desirable, the result of conditions that are functional for the persistence of society. Although the point is dealt with briefly toward the end of the paper, an analysis of this aspect of his work is beyond the scope of the present discussion.

apart from the fact that it may be consistent with a given body of facts. This is especially true, we think, of analyses that attempt to draw out the implications of a given position for social change as a solution to some problem. Indeed, it may be that the implications for change are among the most important features influencing the acceptance of a given theoretical position.

Durkheim: The Concept of Crime

Durkheim's most elaborate treatment of the concept of crime appeared in *The Division of Labor* (1964b). In that work, Durkheim made the now well-known distinction between mechanical and organic solidarity. It will be recalled by students of his work that mechanical solidarity exists when persons are held together by a collective conscience, conceived as a set of specific moral norms and supporting sentiments with respect to which there is a high degree of consensus. Organic solidarity exists when people are held together by the functional interdependence that develops when roles are specialized. It will be recalled also that the former is characteristic of the simple societies and the latter of the more advanced or modern societies.

In developing his concept of crime, Durkheim points out that each of the types of solidarity that he distinguishes gives rise to a particular type of law. Mechanical solidarity gives rise to repressive law and organic solidarity to restitutive law. Because they offend the collective conscience, violations of repressive law result in punishment and are conceived as crimes. In his own words (1964b:80): "We can, then ... say that an act is criminal when it offends strong and defined states of the collective conscience." Violations of restitutive law, on the other hand, result in efforts to restore the status quo ante and are conceived as torts. The latter are essentially violations of contract. More specifically, they are agreed on in terms of contract that relate specialists in a society characterized by organic solidarity.

Because by definition crime is associated with the collective conscience, it might be inferred that crime appears only in the simpler societies and disappears with the development of modern societies. Such an interference would be justified if the collective conscience could be said to disappear with the development of organic solidarity. Our interpretation of Durkheim compels us to conclude that it does not, that the collective conscience persists in modern societies, even though the principal basis of solidarity is the functional interdependence of work roles and the contractual relations that tie them together.

Durkheim's position on the existence of a collective conscience in modern societies may be seen in his criticism of the view, held by the early political economists, that integration in such societies if the result of a network of essentially economic contracts between formally free individuals in a market. He argued that this could not possibly be the case, because contracts would be quite impossible without prior commitment to a set of rules of the game. Contractual relations, in other words, presuppose a normative structure without which the formation of such relations could not proceed in an orderly fashion. Thus, although functional interdependence is a central feature of organic solidarity, there is more to it than this. It involves an appropriate set of rules for ordering the contractual relations involved.

> If the division of labor produces solidarity, it is not only because it makes each individual an exchangist, as the economists say; it is because it creates among men an entire system of rights and duties which link them together in a durable way. Just as social similitudes (in the simpler societies) give rise to law and morality which protects them, so the division of labor (in modern societies) gives rise to rules which assure pacific and regular concourse of divided functions (1964b:406).

It seems reasonable to conclude, then, that the development of organic solidarity does not involve the disappearance of a collective conscience, but rather the emergence of a new collective conscience, one that is compatible with the presumably more suited to the needs of modern societies.[2]

---

2. An important modern scholar who has elaborated on and employed Durkheim's work in this regard is Kai Erickson, in his "Notes on the Sociology of Deviance" (Erickson, 1962).

The discussion of Durkheim's views on the development of organic solidarity is important in several respects. If it is valid to conclude that a collective conscience (albeit of a different kind) exists in connection with organic solidarity, then it may be argued that there are elements of mechanical solidarity even in modern societies. More important for present purposes, it may be argued (using Durkheim's definition of crime as a serious violation of the collective conscience) that crime is no less likely to be found in modern societies than in the simpler ones.

Durkheim: The Inevitability of Crime

Durkheim's most compelling argument for the inevitability of crime in human societies is to be found in *The Rules of Sociological Method* (1964a).[3] It should be noted that Durkheim's concern in *The Rules* is not with showing that crime is inevitable but rather with showing that it is "normal." But it is clear from the text of his work that by "normal" he means "inevitable." Early in his discussion of the subject (1964a), he states: "In the first place crime is normal because a society exempt from it is utterly impossible" (p. 64). It is clear also that he has not altered his concept of crime. It remains an act that offends strong and defined states of the collective conscience. In summary form, his argument concerning the inevitability of crime is as follows:

> In a society in which criminal acts are no longer committed, the sentiments they offend would have to be found without exception in all individual consciousnesses, and they must be found to exist with the same degree as sentiments contrary to them. Assuming that this condition could actually be realized, crime would not thereby disappear; it would only change it form, for the very cause which would thus dry up the sources of criminality would immediately open up new ones (1964a:64).

In more elaborate terms, Durkheim is arguing that society is

---

3. For an elaboration of this view, see Parsons' *The structure of Social Action* (1949:324-338). There is one difference between the view expressed by Parsons and our own. Parsons sees Durkheim as having come to the conclusion some time after publishing *The division of Labor.* We see it in *The Division of Labor* as well as his later work.

a moral order, which means its boundaries are defined by moral norms and that, insofar as this is the case, what is defined as crime at any given time can be eliminated only by the most successful kind of socialization. For example, the sentiments underlying any particular law would have to be implanted uniformly in all individuals and with an intensity sufficient to deter the expression of all desires to the contrary, a goal that he considered impossible of attainment:

> A uniformity so universal and absolute is utterly impossible; for the immediate physical milieu in which each one of us placed, the hereditary antecedents and the social influences vary from one individual to the next, and consequently diversify consciousness. It is impossible for all to be alike, if only because each has his own organism and that these organisms occupy different areas in space (1964a:69).

More fundamentally, even if it were possible through a process of socialization to eliminate those acts defined as crime at any given time, the very process by which this is accomplished would create new categories of crime.

> One easily overlooks the consideration that these strong states of the common consciousness cannot be thus reinforced without reinforcing at the same time the more feeble states, whose violation previously gave birth to mere infraction of convention–since the weaker ones are only the prolongation, the attenuated form, of the stronger. Thus robbery and simple bad taste injure the same single altruistic sentiment, the respect for that which is another's. However, this same sentiment is less grievously offended by bad taste than by robbery; and since, in addition, the average consciousness has not sufficient intensity to react keenly to the bad taste, it is treated with greater tolerance. That is why the person guilty of bad taste is merely blamed, whereas the thief is punished. But, if this sentiment grown stronger, to the point of silencing in all consciousness the inclination which disposes man to steal, he will become sensitive to the offences which, until then, touched him but lightly. He will be the object of greater opprobrium, which will transform certain of them from the simple moral faults that they were and give them the quality of crimes (Durkheim, 1964:168).

Put in other words, the argument is as follows: By strengthening the sentiments underlying the law (e.g., respect for the property or the person of another), the result may very well be a reduction in the number of acts that offend these sentiments, from the most serious (those considered crimes) to the least serious (those considered "simple moral faults"). But as a consequence of the very same change (i.e., strengthening the sentiments underlying the law) there will be another outcome as well; the definition of what is criminal will change in the direction of including acts that were before simple moral faults. Thus, if crime is conceived as a serious violation of the collective conscience, it cannot be eliminated by strengthening the grip that such conscience has on the group.

Quinney: Society, Law and Crime (Phase 1)

Quinney's conclusions on the question of the inevitability of crime can be seen in two of his works that deal with the relationship between crime and society. In the first of these works, *The Social Reality of Crime* (1970), his conclusion is quite consistent with Durkheim's, that is, he seems to suggest that crime in modern societies is inevitable, although he arrives at the conclusion by a route that differs rather radically from that developed by Durkheim. In the second publication, *Critique of Legal Order* (1974), Quinney's conclusion is not at all consistent with that of Durkheim. We present both lines of reasoning so as to show how they differ and also to show how his general conceptual scheme differs from that of Durkheim. An examination of Quinney's concepts of society, law, and crime should make these differences evident.

For Quinney, society is conceived as highly segmented, which means that it is characterized by heterogeneity of organization from one segment to another in terms of values, norms, and ideology. He states:

> Underlying this theory of crime is a conception which for consistency, I will refer to as the *segmental organization* of society. This conception is in sharp contrast to the singular, one value system, conception of society (Quinney, 1970:208).

Each of the segments of society may be said to have its own interests in terms of which it may or may not act. Such interests are a function of the cultural tradition of the segment. Quinney (1970) remarks:

> Each segment of society has its own values, its own norms, and its own ideological orientations. When these are considered to be important for the existence and welfare of the respective segments, they may be defined as interests.... Thus, interests are grounded in the segments of society and represent the institutional concerns of the segments (p. 38).[4]

It seems clear that Quinney does not deny the existence of institutionalized normative patterns. However, such patterns as exist are found for the most part within the various segments of a society and not between them. Even where it can be demonstrated that a normative pattern is shared by two or more groups that are otherwise segmented this does not deny the reality of segmentation. In any case, it is not the elements of culture that are shared by various segments of a society that are significant for the development of criminal law, as we shall see, but those that are not.

Quinney considers two general types of interest orientation. The first he refers to as "formal interests," which consist of those policies or activities that are beneficial to the segment but that are not being acted on, perhaps because the members do not recognize them as such. This is the type of interest involved in Marx's concept of class in itself and Dahrendorf's concept of a latent interest group.[5] The second type of interest orientation is referred to as "active interests." These are not only manifest to the members of a segment but actively being pursued by them. This is the type of interest involved in Marx's concept of "class for itself" and in Dahrendorf's "manifest interest group." It is the "active interests" with which Quinney is primarily concerned, for

---

4. Quinney's concept of "segment" appears to be close to Durkheim's concept of "society." But as we shall see, Quinney does not allow for the possibility of "crime within the segment."

5 See Dahrendorf's *Class and Class Conflict in Industrial Society* (1959).

it is in the process of pursuing them that public policy, including the criminal law, may be affected.

But if active interests determine a segment's orientation in the process of public policy making, it is power that determines the outcome of that process. Thus, says Quinney (1970), "Wherever men live together conflict and a struggle for power will be found" (p. 11). Moreover, power will be unequally distributed, for not all who participate in the struggle can be winners.[6]

So that there is no misunderstanding of the radical quality of his conception of Law, Quinney contrasts his views with those of Roscoe Pound. Pound sees law in terms of a "pluralistic consensual" model of society. That is, while he recognizes a plurality of individual and group interests in society he sees a consensually held law as regulating the conflict which is inherent in this pluralism.[7] Thus law is viewed as operating in the public interest. In discussing the conception of law, Quinney (1970) related the following statement:

> In recent juristic language, law functions "first to establish the general framework, the rules of the game so to speak, within and by which individual and group life shall be carried on, and secondly, to adjust the conflicting claims which different individuals and groups of individuals see to satisfy in society"[8] (p. 33).

Law, from this point of view, is something that is shared and with respect to which there is considerable commitment. In the language characteristic of modern sociology, Pound's conception of law is normative, which means that it is an institutionalized element in the relations between interacting parties. At the same time, it should be clear that the pluralists recognize the existence

---

6. Quinney subscribes to a traditional concept of power. It is, simply put, the ability of individuals or groups to exercise control over other individuals or groups. As such it is the principal means of pursuing one's interests, whatever they may be. Should the pursuit of one's interest require the establishment of criminal law, power then becomes the principal means for determining what acts shall be defined as crimes.

7. The conflict inherent in plural society is regulated (if not resolved) by a body of law widely shared by the members of the society and felt to be necessary for the effective functioning of the society.

8. The quotation is from an article by Carl Auerboc, "Law and Social Change in the U.S." (1959:516-532).

of conflict in society. However, law is viewed as a mechanism by which the conflict is resolved. Its capacity to function in this manner necessitates that it be an object of joint commitment in a world that may be otherwise filled with conflicting values and interests.

Quinney's view of society does not admit to the notion that law is normative, as the pluralists suggest. The distinctiveness of the two views revolves about the characterization of the relations between the various sectors of society. Although the pluralist imagery finds law to be the consensual cement that binds otherwise diverse groups, the "segmentalist-conflict" imagery finds the relevant groups of society fundamentally separated from one another. At least there is no consensus that is relevant to the matters of law and crime. This is not to say that law does not emerge in this contest. Indeed, the conflict view of the law suggests that it is precisely in the context of fundamental disconsensus in which groups attempt to regulate each other legally. Law, at its origin at least, is not an element of society over which there is consensus. On the contrary, law is an instrument of coercion, emerging in the context of fundamental conflict and imposed, as it were, on the behavior of subordinate groups. This occurs in an attempt to maintain and coerce patterns of conduct consistent with the values and interest of the superordinate.

It appears then that Quinney's view of the law is in certain respects almost diametrically opposed to that of Pound as well as that of Durkheim. Whereas Pound suggests that the law is associated with normative elements, with respect to which there is considerable agreement, Quinney's position is that where there is agreement there is no need for law, and therefore there is no law. Persons or groups who possess interests in common do not require law to regulate their relations. Law emerges only in areas of disagreement, that is, in those areas in which the interests of persons and groups are in fundamental conflict and are not regulated normatively. There is no doubt then that Quinney understands law and custom as existing within antithetical social milieus. Durkheim's view was, of course, the opposite,

"Normally, custom is not opposed to law but is, on the contrary, its basis" (1946b:65).

To further clarify the issue involved in the distinction between these two concepts of law, it might be useful to examine another distinction, that between norms and rules.[9] The basic difference between them has to do with the question of whether the values involved are shared and internalized (i.e., institutionalized in the relations between the interacting parties). If they are, then both parties are not only aware of them but oriented toward one another in terms of them. When this is the case, the interaction may be described as governed by norms. On the other hand, if the patterns involved are not shared and internalized by the interacting parties, but rather imposed by one party on the other, then the interaction may be described as governed by rules. Clearly, Quinney conceives of the law as a set of rules, rather than a set of norms, for the patterns involved are viewed as imposed by one party on the other.

Before continuing, it might be noted that for Quinney the existence of norms internal to the various segments explains the fact that there is on law internal to the segments, for where values are shared and internalized there is no need for law. It also explains intersegmental conflict, for if the values were not shared and internalized within segments, the attitude toward those of a different persuasion (those outside the segment) would be one of indifference.

Quinney: Society, Law and Crime (Phase II)

Quinney's position on the concepts of society, law, and crime is complicated by the fact that it has changed, in some respects

---

9. The latter is still under development in sociology and for that reason not widely shared. It is our view that functionalists generally employ the concept of *norm* in their analysis of deviant behavior, whereas labeling theorists employ the concept of *rule*. The distinction is crucial in understanding the divergence of these two approaches to deviance. We may consider Durkheim a functionalist in this respect and Quinney as sharing important aspects of the labeling approach. For a discussion of the relation between norm and rule see Wright and Randall (1978).

markedly, between the time he wrote *The Social Reality of Crime* (1970) and the time he wrote *Critique of Legal Order* (1974). The present section deals with these changes.

Quinney begins his critique of legal order (in capitalist society) by noting what has long been taken for granted in sociology, that the methodology of science (to which modern sociology is generally committed) has certain limitations. For example, it cannot tell us what is good and bad in an ultimate sense, but only may shed light on what is true or false. He then proceeds to tell us that by accepting the methodology of science in our efforts to understand society, we are not likely ever to solve the problem of crime. Why? Because even if it provides us with a certain amount of understanding, it does not provide us with answers to the more important question, for Quinney, of what is good and bad or with the motivation to act on what we know, in this case to solve the problem of crime. We question the validity of this conclusion (for reasons that we do not care to take up at this time), but for Quinney it leads to the further conclusion that therefore we must abandon the perspective of science in favor of a "critical philosophy" that commits us to act as well as to understand.

In developing his position in this regard, he rejects the "positivistic mode of thought" as absolutely unacceptable, because of its tendency toward reification. The "social constructionist mode of thought" (which in combination with conflict theory is the dominant orientation of his early work is somewhat more acceptable because it calls attention to reification and in doing so paves the way for change. But insofar as it does not actually commit us to action, it is an insufficient basis for problem solving. Phenomenology, according to Quinney, has a good deal to commend it in that it enjoins us to attempt to transcend our experience in an effort to perceive the essence of things. This is a necessary step, he argues:

> as we begin to act in a way that will truly reveal the social world. Our primary interest is not in the development of a new social science (which would still be a reified science) but in the creation of a new existence, an existence free of all reifications (1974:10).

But even phenomenology is not a sufficient basis for problem solving, for as with the social constructionist mode of thought, it does not commit us to action. For the kind of commitment that Quinney seeks, only a critical philosophy will suffice.

A critical philosophy, Quinney tells us, "is one that is radically critical" (1974:11). It is radically critical in at least two respects. Like the social constructionist and phenomenological modes of thought, it leads us to question the most fundamental assumptions of the social order in which we live. But beyond this it asks us to think of alternatives, not only as a better way of achieving understanding of what exists, but as a way of developing ideas as to what things could be like. Because of these considerations, he then draws what for him is a compelling conclusion: "A critical philosophy must ultimately develop a Marxist perspective" (1974:13).

The most important propositions that make up this perspective and that his critique attempts to defend are as follows:
1. American society is based on an advanced capitalistic economy.
2. The state is organized to serve the interests of the dominant economic class, the capitalist ruling class.
3. Criminal law is an instrument of the state and ruling class to maintain and perpetuate the existing social and economic order.
4. Crime control in capitalist society is accomplished through a variety of institutions and agencies established and administered by a governmental elite, representing ruling class interests, for the purpose of establishing domestic order.
5. The contradictions of advanced capitalism–the disjunction between existence and essence–require that the subordinate classes remain oppressed by whatever means necessary, especially through the coercion and violence of the legal system.
6. Only with the collapse of capitalist society and the creation of a new society, based on socialist principles, will there be a solution to the crime problem (Quinney, 1974:16).

In the process of moving toward a Marxist position, Quinney makes several important changes in his concepts of society, law, and crime. First, society is still segmented, but the number of segments has been reduced to two, the owners of the means of production and the workers. Second, although segmentation is still based on interests, the interest structure is now considerably more focused than before. There are those interests that related to the perpetuation of the capitalistic system and those that do not. Underlying the conflict of interest between the two major segments is the disjunction, in Quinney's terms, between existence and essence, between the existing system of capitalistic production and the essence of humanity that is pressing constantly for fulfillment.[10] Third, criminal law is not simply a

---

10. In taking this position on the source of the conflict of interest in capitalistic society, Quinney seems to have abandoned the voluntaristic theory of action that played such a prominent part in his early work. By postulating an essence that is pressing for fulfillment, he may be said to have adopted one of the several versions of the "positivistic theory of action" described by Parsons (1949). More specifically, we are saying that in suggesting that the ends of action are rooted in the person's essence, Quinney can no longer be said to be a voluntarist. The problem Quinney faces seems to be grounded-in the fact that he wants to see man as capable of creating whatever kind of world he wants, but at the same time destined to be unhappy with the existence that does not permit the fulfillment of his essential nature. In summary, the position implied in his later analysis may be said to be positivistic to the extent that the direction of history is not a matter of voluntaristic choice, but is given in the "nature of things." All that remains to be done is to discover what the nature is and then organize society in such a way as to permit its fulfillment. In Parsons' terms "either the active agency of the actor in the choice of ends is an independent factor in action, and the end element must be random; or the objectionable implication of the randomness of ends is denied, but then their independence disappears and they are assimilated to the conditions of the situation, that is to elements analyzable in terms of nonsubjective categories" (1949:64). To further clarify what we think is an important aspect of Quinney's position, his radical critique established on the basis of the "giveness of ends" (and one that we have called positivistic) is characterized by C. Wright Mills as follows. Mills suggests that according to some radicals,

> For radical criticism to have any meaning it must utter its judgments from some moral norm that transcends the system or from some standard which recognizes an imminent, unfulfilled potential in the existing state of things.

Mills continues to say, distinguishing himself from such scholars as Quinney and clarifying the voluntaristic position:

> I want to make very clear that insofar as this is the meaning I am not a radical critic and never have been. I have never found either a transcendent or an imminent ground for moral judgment. The only moral values I hold I got from right inside history. (Mills, 1971:246).

device for controlling the activities of the less powerful segments of society, although it is this. It is a device for perpetuating the capitalistic system and its principal beneficiaries, the owners of the means of production. The state is thus conceived not only as a mechanism for enforcing the criminal law, but as a creature of the ruling (capitalist) class. Last and perhaps most important, the intersegmental conflict that in his early writing was conceived to be characteristic of all modern societies, is now conceived as capable of being eliminated through a process of social change, specifically by adopting socialist principles of social and economic organization.

Several of the above points require elaboration. In abandoning the concept of society as involving a variety of active interest groups in favor of one involving but two such groups, Quinney does not ignore the wide variety of interests that are competing for representation in law. What he argues is that in one way or another they relate to the class struggle: "Even when laws regulating morality are made and enforced: the intention is to preserve the moral and ideological basis of capitalism" (1974:56). Second, in saying that the state is a creature of the ruling class, (Quinney is speaking literally):

> The state is established by those who desire to protect their material basis and who have the power (because of material means) to maintain the state....Moreover, the legal system is an apparatus created to secure the interests of the dominant class...law is a tool of the ruling class (1974:52).

Equally important, Quinney argues that although the state may be conceived as a tool for the creation of order in a situation in which order is lacking, it may also be conceived as responsible for the disorder in the first place:

> [A] legal order became necessary only when the state broke down communal solidarity and divided the group into conflicting factions. In early states, crimes were invented to serve the needs of the state; that is legal sanctions were needed to protect the new interests of the emerging state. Rather than healing any breaches of custom, law protected the sovereign. The state necessarily broke up customary

patterns, in the interest of economic and political dominance, and instituted a legal system to enforce its sovereignty.

With this understanding of the legal order, we begin to see that law is the antonym rather than the synonym of order (1974:190).

The meaning of the last sentence must be understood in terms of the conflict model within which Quinney's work is set. Even though in terms of that model it may be said that coercion produces order, the order that results is "imperfect" in that compliance is not based on legitimacy. In short, insofar as the state is responsible for the conflict, it may be said to contribute to the disorder that it then attempts to solve.

Quinney: The Inevitability of Crime

Quinney does not elaborate his position on the inevitability of crime. However, it is possible, we think, to infer his view on the question from his statements on the nature of society, law, and crime. As already indicated, his views on all three have changed over time. More important, his views in each of the two periods covered in our analysis can be seen as leading to two different conclusions on the question. In the early period, he states explicitly that "in any society conflicts between persons, social units, or cultural elements are inevitable" (1970:9). Given his view that criminal law is rooted in such conflict and that crime is defined by law, then it can be inferred that crime in inevitable. In the latter period, he concludes that there is at least one type of society in which conflicts of interest can be eliminated, that implied in the Marxist analysis of socialist principles of social and economic organization. Briefly, the argument is as follows: Socialism will eliminate the inequality in the distribution of the material basis for power, namely the means of production, and in the process make the domination of one group by another impossible. At the same time, socialism will eliminate the contradiction "between what exists and what is authentically human" (1974:14). In doing so, it will eliminate the ultimate source of the conflict that now obtains in capitalist society. Given his view that criminal law is rooted in such conflict and that crime is defined by law, then it can be inferred that under certain conditions, crime is not inevitable. Indeed, in Quinney's later work he does make it clear (although he does not elaborate his views on the question) that he does not think much of the position that finds crime an inevitable feature of social life:

> The conventional economic (sic) analysis of crime also assumes the functional inevitability of crime. In viewing crime in functional terms, this kind of analysis leads to the absurd position of seeing crime as a necessary feature of society (1977:191).

Exactly what form the new order (socialism) will take is admittedly not clear, even to Quinney. Presumably, the form will be worked out in the struggle to eliminate the old order. He does argue that the new society, free from conflict and segmentation, will be based on custom rather than law. An illustrative case is the type of community emerging in Cuba:

> A contemporary experience that gives support to the possibility of community custom is the case of revolutionary Cuba. The alternative to national law in this case, and a transitional move to the abolition of law, is the emergence of the popular tribunal. Neighborhoods in Cuba now have their own courts, staffed by personnel elected democratically from within the neighborhood. Custom plays an educative role within the community, rather than a punitive one. What is important is maintaining peace and understanding in the community rather than enforcement of a legal system (Quinney, 1974:191).

Finally, rather than describe for us the form that the new society will take, Quinney asks us to learn by imagination: "We must envision and promote the new society that will emerge in this struggle (with the old order)" (1974:168).

Durkheim and Quinney: Summary Comparison

It should be evident by now that the positions of Durkheim and Quinney on the inevitability of crime are indeed a function of their respective conceptual schemes and the reasoning that they bring to bear in answering certain theoretical questions. Beginning with the conception of crime as serious violation of widely shared (consensual) elements of the normative structure (the collective conscience), Durkheim argues first that crime is the result of the fact that society is an imperfect moral order. This in itself, however, does not mean that crime is inevitable. Because the moral norms that go to make up the collective conscience might conceivably be so thoroughly implanted as to virtually overcome all tendencies to contravene them, his theory of crime appears to allow for the possibility that crime could be eliminated by an unusually successful effort to strengthen the grip that the collective conscience has on the members of the society in which it is found. But all hope for "success" in such an endeavor is dashed when he points out that whatever reduction in violations of the collective conscience effected by such a move would be offset, so to speak, by the introduction of new categories of crime, the latter being the result of the very same process by which the grip of the collective conscience is strengthened. Thus, if crime is a result of the fact that society is an imperfect moral order and furthermore that efforts to strengthen the grip of the collective conscience are self-defeating, crime is inevitable.[11]

Quinney's view is clearly different. Beginning with conception of society as segmented and of law as an outgrowth of the conflicts of interest involved in the relations between segments, the conclusion with respect to the inevitability of crime is inescapable–crime is inevitable. One need not come to this conclusion, however, if it can be shown that some forms of social organization will eliminate the segmentation. This is what Quinney attempts to do in his later work. The mechanism by which it is to be done is Marxist analysis; the operating principles of the new society are to be those of socialism. Furthermore, the kind of society he envisions is in many respects like the simple societies of an earlier period in the history of the western world, those characterized by

---

11. It should be noted that Durkheim is not arguing that crime is functional as some modern theorists (e.g., Erickson, 1962) have suggested, but rather that it is inevitable without regard to its functional significance. Durkheim, in a following statement (1964a) does argue that punishment is functional, but this is a far cry from the suggestion that crime is functional.

Durkheim as involving a collective conscience based on similitudes (mechanical solidarity). But contrary to Durkheim, Quinney does not view social similitudes as giving rise to crime. Rather, crime arises only when the collective conscience breaks down. In the language of modern sociology, crime is not a function of consensus (Durkheim) but a lack thereof (Quinney), which in the case of western societies is due to capitalist social organization. It appears then that the condition seen by Quinney as the solution to the problem of crime is for Durkheim the condition in human social life that makes crime inevitable.

Implications for Change

If our analysis is correct, it goes without saying that Durkheim's views on the nature of crime and society leave us with no hope whatever for the elimination of crime from human society, regardless of what we do. On the other hand, given Durkheim's views, it is possible to change the character of crime. This can be done in one of two ways, by changing the content of the established normative pattern or by strengthening the grip of the collective conscience. Concerning the first of these approaches, it should be obvious that because crime is defined by the collective conscience, any change in the content of its norms will change the character of crime. Concerning the second, strengthening the grip of the collective conscience, not only does such a move reduce the number of violations of what at any given time is defined as crime, it also produces a redefinition of what is criminal to include acts that were before "simple moral faults." Again, such a move would involve a change in the character of crime.

For those who might consider the latter chance as desirable (on the assumption that we would be better off if the frequency of acts that are now defined as crimes were reduced), Durkheim has an important message: It is possible to institutionalize a culture pattern so thoroughly as to make adjustments to changing life conditions (or for that matter, any adjustments) difficult. For Durkheim, a certain level of flexibility is necessary for change to take place and, to the extent that change is imperative for the continued existence of a social group, necessary for survival.[12] Clearly, Durkheim's conceptualization of crime and contingent understanding of the phenomenon does not permit Quinney's optimism.

Again, if our analysis is correct, Quinney's early views on the nature of crime and human social organization leave us with little hope for the elimination of crime from human society. Beginning with the assumption that segmentation is a universal feature of organization at the level of society and that the criminal law is a function of segmentation, we are left with the conclusion that crime is inevitable. Thus his early work leads to the same conclusion that Durkheim arrived at in *The Rule of Sociological Method*, but by a different route. Quinney's later views, on the other hand, leave us with the conclusion that there is a great deal of hope for the elimination of crime from human society. But if there is hope in this regard, the process by which that hope is to be realize is not an easy one, for involved in the processes of change is struggle between the competing segments of modern society. It is here, in connection with the struggle, that a critical philosophy becomes imperative, for without such a philosophy we would have neither the imagination nor the motivation necessary for effective participation.

As indicated earlier, the outcome of the process will be a society based on custom rather than law, which means that order will be a function of institutionalized norms rather than coercion. This line of reasoning, it might be added, does not suggest that somehow deviant behavior will be eliminated but only that such behavior will no longer be illegal, for its parameters will not be defined by law. In the simplest terms, Quinney sees a solution to the problem of crime by eliminating the conditions that generate law and thus the instrument by which crime and the criminal are created.

In closing, a paper such as this suggests a number of direc-

---

12. It should be noted here, lest there be some confusion, that it is not crime that Durkheim finds functional, but rather "institutional flexibility." As it happens, of course, such flexibility is an outcome of the same general condition that produces a relatively high crime rate, that is, attenuate moral commitment.

tions for future research. One is consistent with the nature of the research contained in this work and involves continuation of the study and analysis of the distinctiveness of the fundamental concepts of theoretical systems. There is no doubt that differences at this level have a direct bearing on the development of substantive, empirical conclusions. Just how crime is conceived, as well as how society, law, and so on are developed with a system of thought, will directly affect the determination of the answer to a whole range of questions, including of course, "Is crime in human society inevitable?" Furthermore, a lack of understanding as to just what the basic concepts of a theory intend may give rise to interminable dialogue between the respective theories' advocates as to the correctness of judgments concerning factual states of affairs. This is not to suggest that all or even most of the disagreements among sociologists are mere problems of communication, only that in some instances of disagreement, particularly across the boundaries of what Kuhn (1969) called "disciplinary matrices," the respective parties may literally not know what the other is talking about. In this connection, the first problem to be cleared away is the problem of translating the specialized languages associated with each theoretical system into a more generalized language that each theoretical group might understand, this is, a more general theory. It is in this light that we propose further examination of the basic concepts of theoretical systems. It is only through such effort that we can understand just what Durkheim or Quinney intended when they speak to the issue of the inevitability of crime in human society. The meaning of such statements will remain opaque (or subject to the grossest misunderstanding) until the broad conceptual concepts in which they are embedded have been carefully explored.

At the same time, insofar as it can be argued that these two theories speak to one another, a number of field researchable questions emerge. Briefly, there seems no doubt that some crime occurs within the context of consensus, because the categories are grounded in the customs of consensual groups, and as Durkheim and modern functionalists would have it such crime cannot be eliminated from social life. On the other hand, we are also convinced that many criminal categories are constructed in the context of fundamental conflict of interests between groups and represent an attempt by the superordinate group to control the behavior of subordinates. However, we are not at all sure just where and when and just what crime is or has been associated with consensus and thus has nothing to do with conflict. Neither are we sure just what crime is the product of something like a colonial situation, that is, involves the clash of opposing cultures, interests, and vast inequities in power. It seems to us that sociologists have done very little research with respect to these questions. Rather, crime has tended to be fundamentally conceived in terms of one set of ideas or the other. The result has been that empirical questions surrounding the problem are at best obscured.

References

Auerbock, Carl
    1959 "Law and Social change in the U.S." *U.C.L.A. Law Review,* 6: 516-532.
Dahrendorf, R.
    1959 *Class and Class Conflict in Industrial Society.* Palo Alto: Stanford University Press.
Durkheim, Emile
    1964a *The Rules of Sociological Method.* New York: Free Press.
    1964b *The Division of Labor.* New York: Free Press.
Erickson, Kai
    1962 "Notes on the sociology of deviance." *Social Problems,* 9:307-314
Kuhn, T.
    1969 *The Structure of Scientific Revolutions.* Chicago: University of Chicago Press.
Mills, C. Wright
    1971 *C. Wright Mills and the Power Elite*, W. Domhoff and H. B. Ballard (eds.). Boston: Beacon Press.
Parsons, T.
    1949 *The Structure of Social Action.* New York: Free Press.
Quinney, Richard
    1970 *The Social Reality of Crime.* Boston: Little-Brown.
    1974 *Critique of Legal Order.* Boston: Little-Brown.
    1977 *Class, State and Crime.* New York: McKay.
Wright, Charles and S. C. Randall
    1978 "Contrasting conceptions of deviance." *British Journal of Criminology,* July:217-231.

Adaptive Structures and The Problem of Order

R. E. Hilbert & Charles Wright

Introduction

The aim of our paper is to expose the Parsonian solution to the "problem of order" and, in the process, correct some of the impressions left by his critics concerning the character of that solution. We argue that Parsons' views on the subject are not well understood, even by thoughtful scholars. We call attention to one such scholar who argued that for functionalists generally and Parsons in particular "Every functioning social structure is based upon a consensus of values among its members" (Dahrendorf, 1957:161). Our interpretation of what Parsons is saying is that order in human societies is not based upon a "consensus of values," if by that phrase is meant "the higher the level of agreement on values, the greater the level of order." We argue that, for Parsons, the institutionalization of a consistently integrated pattern of values requires the development of alternatives which conflict with such a pattern. Thus, it may be concluded that within the Parsonian scheme of things, value-consensus is not even possible. We argue, further, that these alternatives, called "adaptive structures," present a problem of integration with the dominant pattern that can be ignored only at the cost of instability and, possibly, change to a new pattern. Thus, while they are an important part of the solution to the problem of order, they also contribute to the problem. Finally, we argue that, for Parsons, an understanding of these structures can provide clues as to the determinants underlying the functional prerequisites, and should therefore be of considerable interest to the social theorist.

The Problem of Order

The problem of order to which we refer is that posed by Thomas Hobbes. It will be recalled that for Hobbes men are driven by certain "passions" which are given in nature and are thus neither good nor evil. The choice of means for Hobbes is governed by a tendency toward rationality, so that, in pursuing their ends, men will choose the most efficient means available, including if necessary, force and fraud. It follows that interaction could degenerate into a situation in which every man is the enemy of every other man, a "war of all-against-all." With this statement of the problem, Parsons had no quarrel. Indeed, he argued that Hobbes "saw the problem with a clarity which has never been surpassed, and his statement of it remains valid today" (Parsons, 1937:93).

But if Parsons was in agreement with Hobbes on the nature of the problem, he was in substantial disagreement with him on the solution. Again it will be recalled that for Hobbes, precisely because men are rational, they eventually come to see that security in the pursuit of any ends can be purchased only at the cost of constraints over the use of force and fraud. The result is a social contract under which men agree to give up the use of such means. In this way, according to Hobbes, the circumstances leading to a "war of all-against-all" are brought under control.

For our purposes at the moment the exact nature of the contract is not important, although it might be noted that it involves the establishment of an authority figure who has the irrevocable right, where necessary, to use coercion in the enforcement of constraints. What is important is that Parsons disagreed with the logic underlying Hobbes' argument that the element of rationality which dictated the use of force and fraud at some point leads to the control of force and fraud. That argument, according to Parsons,

> involves stretching, at a critical point, the conception of rationality beyond its scope in the rest of the theory, to a point where the actors come to realize the situation as a whole instead of pursuing their own ends in terms of their immediate situation, and then take the action necessary to eliminate force and fraud. (Parsons, 1937:93).

The Parsonian solution, as is now well known, emphasizes the immanent development of a set of normative constraints, rather than the rational formulation of a contract under which men are subject to agreed upon constraints that are ultimately coercive.

The Process of Institutionalization

Whatever the reason for the charge that, for Parsons, society is ordered by value-consensus, we think the charge would not be made if there were a better understanding of what is involved in the process of institutionalizing a pattern of values. It is not simply a matter of taking an agreed upon set of values and implanting them within the members of a society with an intensity sufficient to insure a minimum level of stability. For Parsons the process is complicated by the fact that all societies are subject to certain "functional exigencies," conditions which must be met if the society is to persist as an organized entity. At least one class of such exigencies, the "universal imperatives," is a set of conditions which must be met by *any* society if it is to persist, again, as an organized entity.[1] Equally important, the range of such conditions is considerable, so much so that at one point Parsons argues "the exigencies of a going society are such that it is exceedingly unlikely that any one consistently integrated pattern can cover the necessary range." (Parsons 1951:169) What this means, among other things, is that the model of "perfect integration" to which Parsons often makes reference, in the nature of the case, can never be realized. This is clear in the following statement:

> We may say, then, that if the structure of social systems were solely a function of the "free choices" of their component actors, their main structural outline would be capable of description in terms of the patterns of value-orientation alone, and these in turn would be derivable from cognitive and expressive orientation patterns. The extent to which the structure of social systems is not derivable from cultural elements is therefore a measure of the importance of the determinants underlying what we have called the two classes of "exigencies" or

---

[1] The other class of exigencies, called "imperatives of compatibility," limit the range of coexistence of structural elements in the same society.

"imperatives" to which they are subject in the realistic conditions of their operation as systems. These resultants of these factors may be considered as patterns of deviation from what would be the model of "perfect integration" in terms of the dominant pattern of value-orientation (Parsons 1951:168).

It is clear that the model of "perfect integration," for Parsons, is not a description of reality, but a heuristic device, a point of reference for analysis, and that operating systems of necessity involve departures from such a model.

Adaptive Structures

As indicated earlier, the patterns of deviation to which Parsons makes reference in the above quote are called "adaptive structures." They are defined in relation to the dominant pattern of value-orientation and exist because whatever the dominant pattern may be, if "consistently integrated," it cannot meet all of the needs of an operating system. Thus adaptive structures may be seen as structures which in orientation deviate from the dominant culture pattern, but which are nevertheless important (functionally speaking) to the maintenance of the dominant pattern and the structures in which that pattern is institutionalized.

Precisely because they are functionally important, adaptive structures must be to some degree institutionalized. However, because they are alternatives to the dominant value-pattern, they pose a constant threat to that pattern. It is necessary, therefore, that their legitimacy be conditional and that there be mechanisms in place to minimize interference with the dominant value-pattern. Parsons recognizes the difficulties in doing this and argues that

[T]he problem of integration posed by the necessity of "tolerating" and indeed institutionalizing patterns deviant from the main values is one of the main integrative problems for social systems, the more so, the more complex and differentiated their structure (Parsons 1951:169).

The last general point to be made has to do with the pervasiveness of adaptive structures. For Parsons, one can expect adaptive alternatives to the dominant pattern of value-orientation even in those structures which directly institutionalize the dominant pattern, for example, the occupational and educational systems and within structures, such as an established religion, whose primary function may be to legitimize the dominant pattern. But in addition, for Parsons, there are whole subsystems in which alternatives to the dominant pattern are institutionalized and which qualify as adaptive because they are of crucial functional significance. The clearest examples in the American case is the kinship system.

Adaptive Structures Illustrated

There seems to be little doubt that the dominant value pattern in America today emphasizes universalism and achievement, along with affective neutrality and functional specificity. There seems to be little doubt also that the social structures in which these values are directly institutionalized are the occupational system and the educational system which is so intimately related to it. But even here in these systems there are adaptive aspects, which may be seen as necessary developments given the exigencies of the situation in which the dominant values are being institutionalized. A case in point is the pattern of "seniority" in industry and of "tenure" in the academic world. For Parsons both

> may be treated as adaptive structures which have the function of mitigating the structural strains inherent in the exposure of people to competitive pressures where detailed universalistic discriminations are impracticable. From this point of view such a system is subject to a delicate balance. On the one hand it must resort to adaptive structures which are in conflict with its major value patterns because to push these patterns "to their logical conclusion" would increase strain to the breaking point. On the other hand, it must not let the adaptive structures become too important lest the tail wag the dog, and the major social structure itself shift into another type (Parsons 1951:185).

Another is the existence of certain pseudo-scientific elements in modern medical practice. The focus of Parsons' discussion of the subject is the situation of the surgeon who, faced with a great deal of uncertainty about the efficacy of the technology available to him, must nevertheless decide whether or not to operate.

In part, this is because, as a trained professional, he is expected to act; in part it is because of pressure from the patient and his family, for whom passive inaction, to simply "wait and see what happens," may be difficult to bear. The result is a bias in favor of active intervention.[2]

This bias can be seen also in the pattern of "fashion change" or "faddism" in health care, not just among the general population, but among trained professionals. The phenomenon to which these terms refer is the tendency to adopt new medicines and procedures before they have been thoroughly tested. At the same time, because of the dominant culture pattern and its emphasis on scientific technology, a reaction sets in and the bias in a particular case is brought under control. But as a general phenomenon, the pattern persists because at any one time a number of such examples can be observed.

With respect to its functional significance, Parsons refers to Malinowski's thesis on magic among the Melanesians. For Malinowski, magic tends to be found in situations where there is a concern for success of a given activity, e.g., gardening and fishing in the open sea, plus a high level of uncertainty about the efficacy of the techniques available in connection with that activity. This is precisely the kind of situation faced by many health care professionals. Thus, the "optimistic bias" in modern medical practice may be seen as the functional equivalent of magic among the Melanesians. It adapts the actor to the situation he faces by bolstering his confidence in the efficacy of the techniques available to him.

There is no doubt that for Parsons, the phenomenon qualifies as an adaptive structure in that it involves a departure from the dominant culture pattern, but nevertheless has positive functional significance for the maintenance of that pattern. There is no doubt also that he sees such departures as disruptive, but less so than

---

[2]In his treatment of the subject, Parsons is quick to point out that in an "individual fee-for-service practice the surgeon has a direct financial incentive in favor of operating," but that this does not preclude the existence of other possible motives for the same pattern of behavior (Parsons, 1951:467).

the alternative, e.g., an idealistic effort at consistency. In his own words:

> The general tendency is to fall considerably short of living up to the full "logical" implications of the dominant culture pattern in certain crucial respects. It is suggested that this derives from the fact that it is not possible to "apply" the dominant culture pattern literally and without restriction and not generate strains which in turn would produce responses which would be more disruptive than certain "mitigations" of the rigorous applications of the pattern itself (Parsons, 1951: 470),

Another illustration of an adaptive structure and one about which Parsons himself had a good deal to say is the religious response to "evil."[3] The functionalist position on the matter is familiar to most sociologists so it will be dealt with only in very general terms. Whatever the institutionalized pattern of values in a society, the realization of the related expectations is uncertain and uneven. Put another way, the members of a society seldom get what they deserve, contingent upon "doing the right thing." In part this is because the external nature to which men are exposed is "unfriendly" and "capricious" in relation to what they want. In part it is because it is empirically impossible, as Parsons puts it, to integrate any value system with the realities of the situation men face. From what we know about psychology, situations such as this present "problems of adjustment" for individuals and a search for solutions. It is Parsons' position that certain religious beliefs, called "theodicies," are responses to these problems and, when institutionalized, function as ready-made solutions to them. The belief that the books of the moral economy are balanced in the hereafter is a case in point. Most important for our purposes, such beliefs also forestall deviance by solving an incipient problem of order. They answer the question: "Why conform to normative expectations, if to do so is not rewarded; why not deviate, if to do so is not punished?"

As one might expect, such beliefs are particularly common among the "disadvantaged," those for whom expectations for suc-

---

[3]For extended discussions of the subject, see Parsons, 1952 and Parsons, 1951: 163-167).

cess are often frustrated by circumstances (Niebuhr, 1929). Beliefs such as "the meek shall inherit the earth," taken literally among the disadvantaged, may be seen as illustrative. They qualify as adaptive structures, first because they are institutionalized alternatives to the dominant value-pattern emphasizing achievement and the expectation that "the rich and powerful shall inherit the earth" and, second, because they have positive functional significance for the society in which they are located. How? By adapting the disadvantaged to their "lot in life."

Conflict between the dominant culture pattern and the adaptive aspects of religion can be seen in the controversy over the teaching of "creationism" in high school biology classes. Conventional discussion of the conflict puts the emphasis on ideological differences between the religious right and the secular left. But clearly it can be seen as more than this, and our understanding of adaptive structures suggests that it is. It can be seen as a conflict between (1) the emphasis on science and technology in the educational and occupational systems in the United States today, based as it is on universalistic-achievement values, and (2) certain established fundamental Christian religious beliefs that directly contradict the current scientific explanation for evolution. They hold that man is not the result of a process of natural selection, but a creation of God. These beliefs qualify as adaptive structures because they are an integral part of the theodicy outlined above. At the same time, such beliefs, however adaptive, present a problem of integration with the pattern of values underlying science and technology in that to push the latter to its logical conclusion would, in Parsons' words, "increase strain to the breaking point," while a failure to control its legitimacy could produce major changes in the dominant value pattern.

The case for adaptive structures as having positive functional significance for the maintenance of the dominant value-pattern can be made also by reference to aspects of the system of social welfare in the United States. Starting with the assumption that the structure of the American occupational system places an emphasis on universalism and achievement, it follows that one should be compensated according to one's contribution in terms of goods and services. However, the situation in which these values are institutionalized includes people who are unable to contribute very much, if anything, in terms of goods and services, either because of age, handicaps or no opportunities for employment. If these people could be ignored, according to the theory, that would be the end of the matter, but they can not, especially in a liberal democracy. For one thing, they themselves or those who care about them can be mobilized to vote or otherwise put pressure on the government to take their interests into account. The result is an operating system which includes alternative structures under which one may get "something for nothing." In Parsonian terms, such structures are departures from the model of "perfect integration" in terms of the dominant structure, but may be seen as necessary to the continued existence of that structure.[4] They are also the focus of a great deal of conflict and dissensus in American society.

Even more than in the case of the system of social welfare, the entire system of kinship relationships qualifies as an adaptive structure in modern societies. Given its emphasis on particularism and ascription, it constitutes a distinct alternative to the dominant pattern in such societies, yet is functionally important to its maintenance. In Parsons own words:

> Thus from the perspective of the institutionalization of a universalistic achievement value system, the kinship structure and the patterning of sex roles should be considered primarily as adaptive structures. There is, however, every indication that they are of such crucial functional significance to the motivational economy of the occupational system itself that their institutionalization is of high strategic importance. They cannot be left uncontrolled, and must in some fashion be integrated with the instrumental system. Because of the fundamental difference of patterning, however, the relation between the two structures is bound to be a major focus of strain in this type of society (Parsons, 1951:187).

---

[4]For an elaboration of this thesis, see Piven and Cloward, 1971

This is an important passage in several respects. First, it calls attention to the fact that the kinship system may not be an adaptive structure in all types of societies. The point is captured in the phrase "major focus of strain in this type of society," namely a modern society and not in, say, a pre-modern "folk" society in which the values of the kinship system are not fundamentally different from those of the larger society. Thus the functional imperative is one of compatibility. Second, by focusing on the "functional significance to the motivational economy of the instrumental system," it calls attention to the fact that activity in the educational and occupational systems of modern societies is meaningful in large part because of its relationship to the kinship system, in modern societies, the nuclear family. Equally important for our purposes, it calls attention to a constant source of conflict in such societies. For example, the kinship system, which is responsible for a great deal of "inequality of opportunity," is functionally important to the persistence of a society whose occupational system, based as it is on universalistic-achievement values, emphasizes "equality of opportunity." Parsons' statement that it is a major focus of strain in "this type of society" may be an understatement.

Concluding Remarks

The focus of our paper is on social structures whose value-orientations deviate from those of the dominant structures of a society, but are nevertheless functional for the maintenance of the dominant structures. Called "adaptive structures," they adapt the dominant structures to the realistic conditions of their existence. The conditions at issue are the determinants underlying the two classes of "exigencies" or "imperatives." Thus, adaptive structures are essential elements in the Parsonian solution to the "problem of order." They are also a pervasive source of conflict and dissensus, especially in modern societies, as has been illustrated above. Thus our conclusion with respect to the charge that for functionalists generally and Parsons in particular "every functioning social structure is based upon a consensus of values among its members" if it has any relevance at all to what Parsons is saying, is at best misleading.

Parsons' analysis of the part played by adaptive structures in his solution to the problem of order, we hasten to add, has value beyond demonstrating the existence of conflict and dissensus in functioning social structures. For example, it can be an important tool for sociologists interested in understanding the determinants underlying the functional prerequisites. That is, through an analysis of adaptive structures and related research, it should be possible to more precisely identify those conditions which must be met for a particular system to survive as an organized entity.

For another, through an analysis of the part played by adaptive structures, it should be possible also to better understand the problems presented by the presence of such structures as well as their absence. Parsons' analysis of the kinship system in modern societies is illustrative. It provides the basis for understanding the strains associated with the presence of a structure which is functionally important as well as the strains associated with its absence. The same point can be made with respect to an analysis of the system of social welfare as an adaptive structure in modern societies. In fact, it already has been in the work by Piven and Cloward, cited earlier.

For still another, an understanding of the part played by adaptive structures can contribute to the sociology of deviance and social control. As noted above, for Parsons all adaptive structures, although treated as conditionally legitimate, are alternatives to the dominant structure of a society, and in that sense deviant. And because they have positive functional significance for the continued existence of a dominant structure must be integrated with it. Thus they constitute a special case of institutionalized deviance that presents problems of control. The reaction to the teaching of creationism in high school biology classes is illustrative. There is a great deal of tolerance for this view as an alternative to evolution so long as it does not pose a serious threat to the latter, for example, by being dealt with side-by-side with evolution as a legitimate alternative. But when it *is* dealt with in this way, controls are much more severe, which is what one might expect. In our view, other patterns of behavior might also be treated as illustrative of institutionalized deviance. "Plea-bargaining" in the American criminal justice system and prostitution come to mind. Both have already been treated as having positive functional significance, although without the benefit of Parsons' analysis of adaptive structures (See Blumberg: 1970 and Davis: 1937).

In addition, an understanding of the part played by adaptive structures in the Parsonian solution to the problem of order might shed light on a whole range of issues of concern to sociologists involving conflict in both ideas and interests. For example, the debate in religious circles over the use of force to resist evil, discussed by Weber (Weber: 1958) as a conflict between an "ethic of absolute ends" and an "ethic of consequences," might be better understood by reference to Parsons' analysis of adaptive structures. It could be seen as a conflict between a utopian ideal, embodied in the doctrine of Christian Love, which denies the use of force to resist evil, and a universal functional exigency, the need for the use of force to resist "evil," both from within a functioning social system and from without. For yet another, the debate in the United States over the necessity for certain measures, such as the Patriot Act, codified after 9-11, could be seen as a conflict between, on the one hand, ideals derived from the United States constitution and embedded in the "rule of law" and, on the other, the necessity, real or imagined, for compromises with these ideals in the interest of survival of the very system whose ideals the act compromises.

Parsons' analysis of the functional significance of adaptive structures may account for some of the criticism of his theories as ideologically conservative. By arguing as he does that the institutionalization of a consistently integrated pattern of values, of necessity, requires compromises with that pattern, one might say that he is offering a justification for those compromises, not just an explanation of their functional importance. This is clearly unfair for there is no good reason to believe that he considers them somehow ultimately right, which is what is implied by the term "justification." Likewise, there is no good reason for arguing that Parsons believes adaptive structures are ultimately good (or bad) because they forestall change. In our view, cognitive statements are not inherently ideological. They become ideological only when invested with meaning beyond the question "what is the state of affairs?" We cannot know if the statements Parsons makes are, for him, invested with meaning in this respect unless he tells us they are, and to our knowledge he has not done so.[5]

Finally, it should be clear that the characterization of Parsons' work as "consensus" or "normative" theory does not capture the complexity of his solution to the problem of order. Moreover, it obscures a number of ideas that could be useful tools for the analysis of the structure of social systems.

References

Blumberg, Abraham S, *Criminal Justice* (Chicago: Quadrangle Press, 1970).

Dahrendorf, Ralf, *Class and Class Conflict in Industrial Society.* (Stanford University Press, 1957).

Davis, Kingsley, "The Sociology of Prostitution," in *The American Sociological Review*, Vol. 2 (October), 1937, pp. 744-755.

Niebuhr, H. Richard, *The Social Sources of Denominationalism,* (Henry Holt and Company, 1929).

Parsons, Talcott, *The Structure of Social Action.* (New York: The Free Press, 1937).

Parsons, Talcott, *The Social System.* (New York: The Free Press, 1951).

Parsons, Talcott, "Religious Perspectives in College Teaching: Sociology and Social Psychology" in Fairchild, H.N. (ed.) *Religious Perspectives in College Teaching* (New York: Ronald Press, pp. 286-337).

Weber, Max, "Politics as a Vocation" in *From Max Weber: Essays in Sociology* by Gerth and Mills. (Oxford University Press, 1958: 77-128).

---

[5] For an elaboration of Parsons' views on this very subject, see TSS, Chapter VIII, especially pages 330-332)

The Command Economy as an Adaptive Structure

Richard E Hilbert & Charles Wright

We open with a discussion of the Parsonian solution to the "problem of order" in human societies, emphasizing the functional significance of "adaptive structures" in that solution. Adaptive structures adapt the dominant structure of a society to the realistic conditions of its existence. We then argue that the Command Economy of World War II is an example of an adaptive structure in that it adapted the American system of free-enterprise capitalism to the threat to its cultural boundaries posed by the Axis powers. Precisely because they are alternatives to the dominant structure, adaptive structures must be institutionalized. But their legitimacy must be conditional, and there must be mechanisms in place to prevent them from becoming the dominant structure, that is, to prevent the "tail from wagging the dog." We deal with both features of the situation surrounding the Command Economy of World War II. Finally, we deal with arguably the most important change in the structure of American society that can be traced to the Command Economy of World War II, the Military-Industrial Complex and the National Security State to which it is related.

In a publication entitled *A Collection of Essays in Honour of Talcott Parsons*, we exposed the Parsonian solution to the "problem of order" in human societies, with an emphasis on the functional significance of adaptive structures in that solution (Hilbert and Wright, 2009). Parsons (1951) argued that order in human societies is basically a function of a pattern of values, which is institutionalized. But in addition and equally important are the "functional prerequisites," those conditions that must be met for a social system to be viable in its present form. For example, all systems must deal with the biological prerequisites of individual life, like nutrition and physical safety, and with the maintenance of their patterns of value, through the socialization of new members and the control of tendencies towards deviance. Likewise, all must deal with organized threats to their cultural boundaries. And because no one pattern of values can satisfy all of the prerequisites of an on-going social system, compromises with that pattern are inevitable. In what is essentially a companion to *The Social System*, entitled *Toward a General Theory of Action* (Parsons and Shils, 1962), it is argued that "every society is shot through with such compromises" (p. 177). When institutionalized along with the dominant pattern, they are called "adaptive structures."[1]

Precisely because adaptive structures are compromises with the dominant pattern of values, it is necessary that the legitimacy of such structures be conditional and that there be mechanisms in place to minimise interference with that pattern. The problem of integration posed by the necessity of tolerating structures that deviate from the dominant pattern "is one of the main integrative problems of social systems" (Parsons, 1951: 169).

An important implication of Parsons's views on the significance of adaptive structures is that a high level of consensus with respect to a given pattern of values is likely to have consequences that would threaten the survival of the system in which it is institutionalized, because one or more of the systemic prerequisites for its survival would not be met. Thus, to argue as some critics have (see, for example, Dahrendorf, 1959) that, for Parsons, order in human societies is a function of consensus and nothing more does not begin to describe his position on the subject. Our reading of Parsons suggests that adaptive structures are critical elements in his explanation for order and the persistence of a particular social system. Our discussion of the significance of the Command Economy of World War II should make this clear.[2]

The dominant pattern of values at issue in our analysis is that which underlies the system of free-market capitalism.[3] The prerequisite at issue is that of "boundary maintenance." In the discussion that follows, it is argued that the Axis Powers in the late 1930s and early 1940s posed a threat to our cultural boundaries that required the establishment of what has come to be known as a Command Economy, in our view, an adaptive structure.

For the record, one of the most important adaptive structures in a modern society such as our own is the kinship system, which emphasizes values that are diametrically opposed to those of the dominant pattern. But there are many others as well: Tenure in the university and other large-scale organizations, the functional alternative for "magic" in modern medical practice, the programme of surveillance initiated by the Patriot Act, and elements of the system of social welfare and so on. The first three of these were discussed at length by Parsons (1951) in *The Social System* (pp. 185, 470) and were dealt with in our paper on the functional significance of adaptive structures (Hilbert and Wright, 2009: 116-18). We also considered the elements of the system of social welfare in America and the programme of surveillance initiated by the Patriot Act (Hilbert and Wright, 2009: 119-20, 122). Most important, Parsons's discussion of the significance of these particular structures makes it apparent that solutions to the "problem of order" cannot be fully understood without reference to adaptive structures.

In that original paper, we also noted the importance of mechanisms that function to prevent an adaptive structure from becoming the dominant structure from which it is a departure, to prevent the "tail from wagging the dog" (Hilbert and Wright, 2009: 116-17). Illustrative of such a mechanism in the United States today is the (low) status of the recipients of social welfare benefits and the practice of pointing out the "moral hazards" associated with the provision of such benefits.[4] In the discussion that follows, we deal with the "mechanisms" in World War II, which functioned to prevent the Command Economy from becoming the dominant structure.

In our view, the Command Economy of World War II is such an obvious example of a structure with adaptive functions that we wonder why Parsons did not discuss it in *The Social System*, which was published after the end of the war, in 1951. One possible explanation, of course as follows: The book may have been written and in the process of being published before the history of the period was fully understood. Another explanation is as follows:

That Parsons did not regard the Command Economy of World War II as sufficiently institutionalized to qualify as an adaptive structure, according to his definition. True, it was regarded as a temporary arrangement, thus to be eliminated after the war, but its major features were established by law and fully accepted as necessary for winning the war, however long that might take.

Regardless of the reason for its omission, it is an example of a structure with adaptive functions that deserves to be exposed, not simply because the United States might not have been able to win the war without it, but because of its success in helping to revive the economy of the Great Depression that even the New Deal was unable to accomplish. Finally, it provides an opportunity to expose the "mechanisms of defence" that functioned to prevent the Command Economy from replacing the economic system that existed prior to the war, that of free-market capitalism, and to discuss its importance as a "watershed moment" in American history, with all that implies in terms of producing lasting changes in the American Way of Life.

Fortunately, we now have available elaborate discussions of the essential features of the Command Economy of World War II, although with no reference to it as an adaptive structure. Moreover, the conclusions about its importance conveyed in these discussions are often entirely consistent with what a sociologist might argue. For example, commenting on the motivation for changes made during the war, the historian John W. Jeffries (1996) writes that "Victory and national survival are the overriding concerns of nations at war; other society values and priorities, sometimes even basic ones, are often secondary, at least for the duration" (p. 14).

When we speak of a "Command Economy," we mean one in which there is a high level of control of economic activity by the elected and appointed officials of a nation state. Command economies existed in other countries as well during World War II, Germany and the Soviet Union being the more obvious examples. But although well established in both countries, in the Soviet Union it was not an adaptive structure by our definition in that it was consistent with the dominant economic system of the country at the time, that of socialism. However, this was not the case in Germany. The Command Economy of Germany was a departure from the dominant system of free-market capitalism that existed prior to the establishment of the military regime of the Third Reich.

By all accounts, the Command Economy in the United States during World War II was a huge operation that grew in size and strength beyond anything that had existed before, not the economy of World War I, nor that of the 1930s New Deal state.

The number of federal civilian employees quadrupled, from some 950,000 in 1939 to 3.8 million in 1945. Expenditures soared 11-fold, from not quite $9 billion to over $98 billion in those same years, from about one-tenth to nearly half the Gross National Product. The power of the executive branch expanded enormously as the government controlled production, materials and labor, rationed goods and set prices, spent and taxed more than it ever had before (Jeffries, 1996: 16).

Mobilization–Part I

As one can imagine, mobilizing the economy for war production was an enormous task. Plants had to be built, expanded, or converted to produce war goods. Raw materials and supplies had to be acquired and delivered to those plants according to appropriate priorities and schedules. Workers had to be matched to the production needs. Civilian supplies had to be produced and allocated in a way that did not detract from war production and that insured basic equity. Wages and prices had to be brought under control in order to avoid ruinous inflation. Money had to be found in order to finance the enormously expensive process of war mobilization and production. Each of these tasks alone was daunting enough, their scope and complex interrelationships amounted to an extraordinary challenge, far beyond what the New Deal had taken on in the 1930s (Jeffries, 1996: 18).

The period from 1939 to 1940 was marked by a succession of agencies concerned with mobilization of the economy, but they were only marginally effective. They were hampered by commitments to existing institutional arrangements, and by people at both ends of the political spectrum. There were anti-statist people on the right who were wary of too much power in the hands of the federal government and liberals on the left who were fearful of a business-dominated economy with little concern for labor. The "political will" necessary for an effective all-out effort at mobilization did not develop until after Pearl Harbor.

The most important of these agencies were (1) the War Resources Board, (2) the Advisory Commission to the Council of National Defence, (3) the Office of Production Management and (4) the Supply Priorities and Allocation Board. Established in the White House was the Office of Emergency Management, which was designed to oversee the efforts of the agencies with more specific functions. Finally, to deal with fair distribution of consumer goods and their prices, as well as the possibility of run-away inflation, the Office of Price Administration and Civilian Supply was established. But while only marginally effective, these early efforts provided the precedents and procedures needed by agencies of the Command Economy that developed after Pearl Harbor.

As one might expect, many of the officials in these agencies were recruited from the ranks of managers in business and industry. In functional terms, this made sense in that they were the people who had the knowledge and expertise needed to mobilize a Command Economy. However, because of their commitment to the institutions of free-market capitalism and their close relations to former colleagues, they were often in conflict with the officials who were associated with the New Deal and who were convinced that more government, not less, was the solution to a variety of social and economic problems. Many of the officials who came from business and industry were "dollar-a-year" men, volunteers who were still on the payrolls of the firms from which they came.

Also, as one also might expect, many owners of the businesses and industries needed for war production were reluctant to cooperate with the effort at mobilization. There was a concern for losing their competitive position in the market for the consumer goods they were producing, and for ending up after the war with a high level of debt and unused capacity, a kind of "depression psychosis" as one historian called it (Jeffries, 1996: 65).

At first the agencies of mobilization used incentives, for example, generous cost-plus contracts, rather than more punitive measures, to motivate compliance with what was considered essential for the war. Secretary of War, Henry L. Stimson, had this to say: "If you are going to try to go to war, or to prepare for war, in a capitalist country, you have got to let business make money out of the process or business won't work" (Jeffries 1996: 21). However, as the Command Economy became more thoroughly established, there was no reluctance to use more punitive measures, for example, the withholding of raw materials from firms that refused to convert to war production. For such firms, it was "either produce what is needed or nothing at all."

In this regard, it is important to note that the Command Economy of World War II was a mixed economy, controlled by the federal government, but greatly influenced by big business, big agriculture and big labor, along with their representatives in Washington, DC. Most important, in the vast majority of cases, the units of production were not owned by the government. In those cases, where the government actually owned and operated a defense plant, the equity interest in it was considered to be temporary, as indeed it turned out to be. All such plants were decommissioned at the end of the war or sold to individuals and firms for a fraction of what they were worth. Thus, the Command Economy in the United States may have functioned like the Command Economy of the Soviet Union, but it was unlike the latter in one major respect: The units of production involved were not owned by the people collectively as in the Soviet Union, but by the people individually.

We will have more to say about all this as we proceed. However, it should be clear that during the period leading up to the war, when the Command Economy was under development, activity of the sort associated with free-market capitalism was already severely curtailed.

Mobilization–Part II

After Pearl Harbor, the power vested in the agencies of mobilization increased significantly. In January 1942, the President created the War Production Board, which was established to control both war production and nonessential activity. Not unexpectedly it faced many of the same obstacles that existed before Pearl Harbor: An institutional framework of free-market capitalism and a reluctance to use negative sanctions in their efforts to get compliance. And there was at first a certain amount of operational inefficiency. For example, contracts were sometimes awarded without due consideration for the existence of available facilities, qualified labor and the availability of raw materials. Eventually, however, problems in this regard were solved when the War Production Board was given the authority to control material allocation and production schedules (Jeffries, 1996: 22).

There was so much power in the hands of the War Production Board that a Kiplinger Newsletter quoted "business-minded men within government" as saying that the War Production Board program represented "the last stand of private enterprise" (Lingeman, 2003: 111). The author then goes on to say,

> [T]o allow industry to compete free enterprise style for steel or machine tools or construction lumber would lead to anarchy, inflation and a nationwide black market. In this area, the government had to become regulator, as well as pump primer, and allocate the materials according to need (Lingeman, 2003: 112).

Nor did the potential for change in the economy go unnoticed by Washington. The *New York Times* reported that there was in Washington "a disposition to inquire into how broadly the war is being used to conceal programs of industrial and social reform of which many elements of Congress and other segments of the Washington population have long been suspicious" (Lingeman, 2003: 344).

A year later, in 1943, President Franklin D. Roosevelt established a new coordinating agency, the Office of War Mobilization, which was given significantly more power of control and coordination than had existed before then in any one agency. Headed by James F. Byrnes, a former senator and United States Supreme Court Justice, the power to coordinate the economy vested in his office led to his being known as the "assistant president" (Jeffries, 1996: 22).

But if Byrnes and his staff had the power to make policy in connection with the effort at mobilization, it was the military procurement officers in the various branches of the War Department–the Departments of the Army and Navy, the Maritime Commission and the Aeronautics Board–who were responsible for carrying out that policy. They were the men, the volunteers from corporate America, who made the important decisions in the day-to-day effort at mobilization. In functional terms, as noted above, this made a great deal of sense in that they knew what was needed, what the military wanted, and they were experienced in dealing with firms in the private sector. And with responsibility, of course, comes power, sometimes a great deal of power. At times, nothing seemed to be beyond their control. For example, when it seemed reasonable to suspend competitive bidding, they did so. When it seemed reasonable to forego anti-trust efforts, they successfully persuaded the administration to do so (Jeffries, 1996: 21). With the establishment of the Office of War Mobilization, the institutionalization of the Command Economy was well under way.

Mobilization of the Civilian Sector

In the period prior to Pearl Harbor, the problems faced by agencies charged with mobilizing the civilian sector of the economy were no different from those faced by agencies charged with mobilizing the military sector: Commitments to free-market principles and institutions, a lack of political will to make the kind of drastic changes that were called for and little experience with the process of mobilization. Not even the experience of World War I and of the New Deal state were of much help.

The need to mobilize the civilian sector became apparent as early as 1939 when the increase in wages and prices threatened to produce ruinous inflation, and when, as a consequence, the distribution of consumer goods appeared unfair to those who lacked the money to purchase them (Jeffries, 1996: 27). Efforts were made to siphon off disposable income, for example, through bond drives, but the inflationary gap persisted.[5] Thus, it became necessary to impose extensive rent and price controls. At the same time, they had to deal with the related problem of producing enough food for the workers of the Command Economy, civilian as well as military.

The problem of food production was dealt with by the War Food Administration. Mobilization in this regard was a huge problem because big farming was well organized, represented by the Farm Bureau Federation and their friends in Congress. The War Food Administration was ultimately successful in solving the problems in this regard, but it was at the cost of enormous profits for big farming and the enhancement of its political clout.

The problem of food distribution was addressed by a system of rationing. But because of the ease with which rationing could be circumvented, for example, by black market activity, the system was difficult to administer.

The problems in this regard were ultimately solved, apparently, because most people agreed that rationing was necessary and tended to comply with the rules voluntarily. The problems presented by the increase in wages and prices were serious and had to be dealt with. The increase in wages was directly related to the shortage of labor that the increase in war production created. The shortage of labor meant that labor was in a position to ask for higher wages and to strike if its demands were not met. In 1941 there were over 4,300 work stoppages involving 2.4 million workers. But after Pearl Harbor, President Roosevelt was able to negotiate a "no-strike/no-lockout" agreement with unions and management, and to establish the National War Labor Board to resolve disputes. Strikes and stoppages fell off sharply in 1942, apparently as a result of negotiations, but also as a result of worker patriotism (Jeffries, 1996: 23).

Compared with big farming, big labor did not do so well. The no-strike/no-lockout agreement left unions without its principal weapon in negotiations with management. Moreover, wages were controlled and labor mobility was restricted by rules which prevented labor from taking advantage of opportunities for higher wages. In many industries, for example, one had to secure a "release" from one's current employer to take a similar position in a competing firm.

The only weapon left to labor was the "wildcat strike." Although work stoppages in general were down after Pearl Harbor, wildcat strikes continued to increase, involving twice as many workers in 1943 as in 1942. The most serious dispute in 1943 arose in the bituminous coal industry. The miners had real grievances: Terrible working conditions and low pay. They also had a charismatic leader in John L. Lewis, who had a record of defying the federal government and the President. However, rather than give in to Lewis's demands, the government took over the mines and forced the men to work. But then later that year President Roosevelt ordered Harold Ickes, his Interior Secretary, to negotiate a contract that was acceptable to Lewis and the situation was stabilized until the end of the war.

Because wartime strikes antagonized the public, the Seventy-eighth Congress was able to enact the War Labor Disputes Act, known as the Smith-Connally Act, after its principal sponsors. The act required unions to provide formal notice of intent to strike, mandated a cooling-off period of 30 days, specified penalties for "illegal" work stoppages, and increased the power of the president to seize war plants that had been struck. It also restricted the right of unions to contribute to political campaigns. Within the Command Economy of World War II, labor was more constrained than big farming or big industry. In many respects, until after the war, the concept of "free labor" no longer described this factor of production.

Conflict and Cooperation: The Case of the Dollar-a-Year Men

Property rights are never unlimited. There are always some things we cannot do with what we "own." What the Command Economy did was to reduce pre-war property rights by specifying what it is one must do in order to be a part of the wartime effort, which is another way of saying to an owner of a vital industry: "Convert, find substitutes–or perish," as one author put it (Lingeman, 2003: 116). This was the case with a number of industries that were needed for war production. The automobile industry, for example, was told "you must produce tanks and airplanes or nothing at all, because raw material will not be available to you otherwise."

And this was not the only restraint or type of "regulation" businesses and industries faced when they were regarded as essential for the conduct of the war. There were regulations with respect to prices and profits, wages and benefits, the quality of what was produced, even cooperation between producers in the interest of overall efficiency. And with each regulation their property rights were, in effect, curtailed. Thus, while it could be said that individuals owned the firms that were mobilized for the war, the rights that they had possessed in the market prior to the war were now greatly reduced, if not completely eliminated. At the same time, they enjoyed huge profits that were virtually guaranteed, so that the problem of securing compliance with the new regulations was not all that difficult.

As noted above, with responsibility comes power, for without power responsibilities could not be carried out successfully. And since it was the procurement officers who had the responsibility for the day-to-day operation of the Command Economy, it was they who had the requisite power. Procurement officers numbered in the thousands and were organized by categories and on several levels of specificity. There were officers concerned with the procurement of airplanes and others with the procurement of warships, and those who dealt with airplanes were broken down into those who dealt with bombers versus those who dealt with transport planes and so on. And this is not all they were responsible for: There were contracts to be negotiated, resources to be allocated and quality to be monitored.

Involved as procurement officers with respect to all of the above categories and at all levels in the Command Economy were the "dollar-a-year" men, described above. What makes them interesting is that they were committed to the principles of free-market capitalism, even as they carried out the policies of the Command Economy. However, because of those commitments they were often in conflict, ideologically, with the professional civil servants, who were said to be sympathetic with the views of the President and the New Deal policies they administered. Marquis Childs is quoted as saying:

> The greatest antagonism was between the avid New Dealers, also called "red hots" and "all outers," and the dollar-a-year men. The New Dealers said bitterly that the dollar-a-year men were only in government to protect the special interests they represented. And the dollar-a-year boys replied that the New Dealers were out to destroy private enterprise (Kennett, 1985: 109).

A comment on the functional significance of the presence of the dollar-a-year men in the Command Economy is in order. First, because the New Dealers with whom they worked were convinced that the regulations introduced in the process of mobilization were the answer to many of the problems of the Great Depression, there was a tendency to see them as ultimately good, not simply as necessary for winning the war. Moreover, the success of the war effort in stimulating the economy presented convincing evidence that Lord Keynes was correct in arguing for an increase in government expenditures as a solution to a sluggish economy. Thus, it would not be an exaggeration to argue that many New Dealers would have been happy to see the Command Economy become the dominant system and that the presence of the dollar-a-year men was an important factor in keeping that from happening, in keeping the "tail from wagging the dog."

There is no reason to believe that the dollar-a-year men were recruited to forestall the institutionalization of the Command Economy as the dominant system in America. But given their commitments to the institutions of a free-market economy, it is reasonable to argue that their presence had that effect. For the record, the dollar-a-year men were a large part of the professional workforce. By one estimate, in 1943, 87% of the men concerned with mobilization and management of the Command Economy were dollar-a-year men (Kennett, 1985: 109).

The Birth of the Military-Industrial Complex

There is a great deal of agreement among scholars as well as the general public that World War II was an important "turning point" in American history, the crucible that forged modern America. Socially, politically, economically, demographically, even sexually, America would never again be the same. "It was the transforming event that shaped all who lived through it, and continues to affect those born after it" (Jeffries, 1996: 3). Entire social movements, such as the women's movement and the civil rights movement can be traced to wartime America. But arguably the most important and certainly the most influential development, economically and politically, that can be traced to World War II is the Military-Industrial Complex and the National Security State, which is dependent upon it.

There has always been a symbiotic relationship between the military and the producers of war material, at least since the beginning of the modern period, when technology became an important element in the success of warfare. The military has relied upon the producers of military hardware in their efforts to protect their national boundaries or their colonies, and the producers of that hardware have relied on orders from the military to survive and prosper.

The experience of World War II provided convincing evidence of the importance of technology. In addition to the atom bomb, there were

> improvements in radar, sonar (which played a apart in breaking the German submarine blockade), the VT proximity fuse, various spe-

cialized types of rocket weaponry, amphibious vehicles such as the DUKW, flamethrowers, medical technologies such as blood plasma and the large scale production and therapeutic employment of Sir Alexander Fleming's penicillin, synthetic drugs such as Atabrine (a substitute for scarce quinine), jet planes, improvements in flight conditions (the pressurized cabin, the anti-G suit to prevent blackouts during pullouts from steep dives) and DDT (Lingeman, 2003: 128).

The symbiotic relationship between the producers of war material and the military gave rise to a number of interests that continued to exist after the threat to our national boundaries subsided. Understandably, leaders of war-related industries were interested in continuing the kind of relationships that had developed between them and the military during the war, those involving, for example, contracts with few of the risks associated with the free-market and profits that were virtually guaranteed. On the other side of the market, as Friedrich Hayek in his 1944 book, *The Road to Serfdom*, pointed out: There were the bureaucrats who, during the war, had "tasted the powers of coercive control and [who] will find it difficult to reconcile themselves with the humbler roles they will then have to play" in the more peaceful times ahead (Lingeman, 2003: 146).

With the end of the hostilities, there was a sharp reduction in the need for the production of war material. Factories were suddenly closed and workers forced to find alternative employment. According to Lingeman, (2003: 357) in the spring of 1945, at Ford's Willow Run plant, "people would simply walk into the office of their housing unit, toss their keys on the table, and drive off to where they came from. Thus, by Christmas of that year, where 13,000 workers had once lived, there were now only about 600 families." At the same time, the disruptive effects of these closings were offset by an expectation that in time the economy would return to some semblance of normalcy. There was even talk of a peace dividend. Unfortunately, (or fortunately, depending on one's values) other wars, the Korean, the Vietnam conflict, and especially the Cold War, created the demand necessary for a Military-Industrial Complex to survive and prosper.

The importance of the Military-Industrial Complex and the part it plays in the National Security State are not to be underestimated. For example, it has become a significant factor both in our economy and in the development of our foreign policy. Indeed, it had become such a large part of the American economy during the Cold War that, as George F. Kennan put it in the preface to Norman Cousins's *The Pathology of Power*:

> Were the Soviet Union to sink tomorrow under the waters of the ocean, the American military industrial complex would have to remain, substantially unchanged, until some other adversary could be invented. Anything else would be an unacceptable shock to the American economy (Cousins, 1987: iv).

Kennan's statement, even if an exaggeration, calls attention to the problem involved in any attempt to bring the Military-Industrial Complex under control. For example, the variety of interests that would have to be dealt with, including, in addition to those of the industries involved, those of the workers in those industries and the communities that have become dependent on those workers for their survival.

Kennan's statement is amplified in a paper by Franklin C. Spinney, entitled *Defense Power Games*. In it, Spinney argues that there are two components to the games: Known in Pentagonese as "front-loading" and "political engineering." Taken together, they constitute two of the most important structural features of the Military-Industrial Complex, and help to explain their persistence over the years since World War II. Both components deviate from what is regarded as the ideal, market-oriented, free-enterprise economic system (Spinney, 1990: 6):[6]

> Front loading is the practice of planting seed money for new programs while down playing their future obligations. This game, which is a clever form of the old-fashioned "bait-and-switch," makes it easier to sell high cost programs to skeptics in the Pentagon and Congress. Political engineering is the strategy of spreading dollars, jobs and profits to as many important congressional districts as possible. By making voters dependent on government money flows, the political engineers put the squeeze on Congress to support the front loaded

program once its true costs become apparent. Front loading and political engineering are about increasing the flow of money; the former starts the money flowing while the latter tries to lock the spigot open, and in American politics, control of the money spigot is power (Spinney, 1990: 7).

In addition, in a letter from the Director of the Military Reform Project of the Project on Government Oversight, dated July 9, 2015, the author argues that:

> Overall, we find some of the most egregious and systemic issues to be inadequate competition, sole-source contracts, the use of risky contract vehicles, and the misuse of commercial items designations that prevent the Department of Defense from getting information about pricing for items that have no real commercial market (Letter on file with the authors).

Finally, with respect to its significance in our economy, "Overall for fiscal year 2017, the Pentagon requested $582.7 billion in discretionary funding, a $2.4 billion increase from last year's enacted level of spending" (Smithberger, 2016: 4) and "if we count related activities like homeland security, veterans' affairs, nuclear warheads at the Department of Energy, military aid to other countries, and interest on the military-related national debt, that figure reaches a cool $1 trillion" (Hartung, 2016: 1).

The Military-Industrial Complex as an Adaptive Structure

Having concluded that the Command Economy of World War II is an adaptive structure and that the Military-Industrial Complex that emerged after the war is a product of that economy, there remains the important question of whether the Military-Industrial Complex of today qualifies as an adaptive structure, an institutionalized pattern of behavior that deviates from the dominant pattern, but that is nevertheless necessary for the continued existence of the dominant pattern from which it deviates.

Clearly, it is institutionalized. The fact that it has existed as a major structural arrangement from World War II to the present attests to this.

Clearly, it is a departure from the dominant system of free-enterprise capitalism. The discussion above supports this conclusion. If additional evidence is needed, one could cite the existence to this day of contracts executed without competitive bidding or with cost-plus arrangements of the sort that were deemed necessary during World War II, when the cost of promising new products was unclear.

Whether it is necessary to the continued existence of the dominant system of free enterprise capitalism is a difficult question to answer. Its defenders claim that it is, but that does not deal with the question of whether it really is, whether in its absence our cultural boundaries would be seriously threatened. What is clear from the record is that calls for reductions in appropriations even at the end of the Cold War, referred to by proponents as a peace dividend, were never implemented. And defenders of the Military Industrial Complex quickly pointed to the necessity for a continuation of current levels of funding in the interest of a strong national defense. The incursions in Kuwait and Iraq that followed provided additional support in this regard. As of August 2015 the Pentagon is asking for an additional $38 billion in order to deal with threats to national security.

There is the possibility, of course, that the Military-Industrial Complex has become such an important part of the American economy that a significant reduction in military expenditures would indeed constitute "an unacceptable shock" to that economy, as George F. Kennan put it (Cousins, 1987: iv). If correct, Kennan is directing us to an adaptive structure that has less to do with the protection of our cultural boundaries, than with its importance in maintaining a high level of economic activity, a consequence of government intervention that a Keynesian economist might argue is necessary to sustain a market-oriented economic system. The constant reference to the Military-Industrial Complex as necessary for our national defence may simply be a useful fiction, what in more elegant sociological terms might be called a functional myth.

Concluding Remarks

The Command Economy of World War II in our judgment is an obvious example of what Parsons calls an "adaptive structure." Its principal features departed significantly from the dominant system of free-market capitalism, but at the same time were regarded as necessary for the ultimate survival of that system and the arguments in support of this conclusion are consistently strong. Finally, it was institutionalized, in that there was widespread acceptance of its principal features and it was supported by law. At the same time, there were mechanisms in place to prevent it from replacing the dominant system.

Whether the Military-Industrial Complex of today qualifies as an adaptive structure is an important question. It has some of the same features as those that characterized the Command Economy of World War II, and for some of the same reasons, they are regarded as necessary for the survival of the dominant system. Whether it really is necessary in this regard is also an important question, but one that cannot be answered with the evidence available to us. Much depends, of course, on the magnitude of the threat to our cultural boundaries that we face at this particular period in time. All we are prepared to say with respect to the threat is that it appears to be much less than that which we faced from 1939 to 1945.

Then there is the possibility, as suggested above, that the Military-Industrial Complex is necessary for the survival of the dominant system for reasons that have less to do with national security than with the survival of its market-oriented economy, a possibility that in our judgment should be seriously considered.

Declaration of Conflicting Interests

The author(s) declared no potential conflicts of interest with respect to the research, authorship, and/or publication of this article.

Funding

The author(s) received no financial support for the research, authorship, and/or publication of this article.

Notes

1. For the theorist interested in the early development of the concept of adaptive structures, a discussion of its essential features can be found in *The Structure of Social Action* (Parsons, 1937). In that work, Parsons argues that all action takes place within situations involving "reality factors" or "conditions of action" that must be dealt with if a society is to survive in its present form.

2. It is our view that the concept of an "adaptive structure" and its theoretical significance in connection with the problem of order in human societies suggests that it is a powerful analytical tool for understanding the sources of strain in such societies and thus the potential for change in the dominant pattern. An adaptive structure may be thoroughly integrated and effectively controlled or it may not, in which case it can result in changes in the dominant pattern. An understanding of such strains and the underlying conditions of action could direct us towards the basic elements of a Parsonian theory of change.

3. It is not unreasonable to question whether the United States in the 1930s is best described as a system of free-market capitalism with an emphasis on competition, given the compromises that had already been institutionalized as adaptive structures prior to and in connection with the New Deal State, but our reference is to the dominant pattern, with respect to which there is considerable agreement among journalists and scholars. There is no doubt about how Parsons felt about the matter. In abstract pattern-variable terms, he argued that "The Universalistic Achievement pattern (the essence of competition) is best exemplified in the dominant American ethos" (Parsons, 1951: 107–08).

4. For an in-depth discussion of the functional significance of the system of social welfare, see Piven and Cloward (1993).

5. Following is an interesting aside: the Kate Smith Bond Drive made no reference to the goal of reducing inflationary pressures; rather, it argued "Buy Bonds and Bring the Boys Home Sooner," an outcome that had no relationship to the purchase of bonds.

6. Spinney is highly regarded as a scholar by the Project on Government Oversight.

References

Cousins, Norman. (1987) *The Pathology of Power.* New York: Norton.

Dahrendorf R (1959) *Class and Class Conflict in an Industrial Society.* Stanford, CA: Stanford University Press.

Hartung WD (2016) The Pentagon's war on accountability. *The Defense Monitor* 45(2): 1.

Hilbert RE and Wright C (2009) Adaptive structures and the problem of order. In: Hart C (ed.) *A Collection of Essays in Honour of Talcott Parsons.* Cheshire: Midrash Publications, pp. 113–123.

Jeffries JW (1996) *Wartime America: The World War II Home Front.* Chicago, IL: Ivan R. Dee Inc.

Kennett L (1985) *For the Duration: The United States Goes to War, Pearl Harbor-1942.* New York: Charles Scribner's Sons.

Lingeman R (2003) *Don't You Know There's a War on.* New York: Thunder's Mouth Press/Nation Books.

Parsons T (1937) *The Structure of Social Action.* New York: The Free Press.

Parsons T (1951) *The Social System.* New York: The Free Press.

Parsons T and Shils E (eds) (1962) *Toward a General Theory of Action.* New York: Harper Torchbooks.

Piven FF and Cloward RA (1993) *Regulating the Poor: The Functions of Public Welfare,* 2d ed. New York: Vintage Books.

Smithberger M (2016) Pentagon's 2017 budget was Mardi Gras for defense contractors. *The Defense Monitor* 45(1): 4.

Spinney FC (1990) *Defense power games fund for constitutional government,* Washington, DC. Available at: http://www.dnipogo.org/fcs/def_power_games_98.htm (accessed 19 January 2016).

Author Biographies

Richard E Hilbert is a Professor Emeritus of the University of Oklahoma (OU). For a number of years prior to his retirement from OU, he served as Chairman of the Department of Sociology. After retiring from OU, he served as a Regents Professor at the University of Science and Arts of Oklahoma. His PhD is from Pennsylvania State University. The subject areas in which he specialized over the years are Deviance and Social Control, The Sociology of Religion, and General Theory. Most of his publications have to do with the Theory of Anomie, its development, and current status. Prior to coming to OU, he taught for seven years at Allegheny College in Meadville, Pennsylvania. Hilbert lives with his wife Lois in Norman, Oklahoma.

Charles Wright holds a PhD in sociology from the University of Notre Dame and a JD (law) from Oklahoma City University. He taught at the University of Oklahoma and Oklahoma City University. His area of specialization is comparative sociological theory. He is also the author of *Constructions of Deviance in Sociological Theory: The Problem of Commensurability* (1984).

www.ingramcontent.com/pod-product-compliance
Lightning Source LLC
Chambersburg PA
CBHW050143170426
43197CB00011B/1946